# I Love You, Clowns Are Scary

Ho'oponopono for Kids and Other People

*Kitty Wells*

*Illustrations by Christie Noe*

**BALBOA**
PRESS

A DIVISION OF HAY HOUSE

Scripture quotations marked KJV are from the Holy Bible, King James
Version (Authorized Version). First published in 1611. Quoted from the KJV
Classic Reference Bible, Copyright © 1983 by The Zondervan Corporation.

Balboa Press books may be ordered through booksellers
or by contacting: www.hooponoponoforkids.com

Balboa Press
A Division of Hay House
1663 Liberty Drive
Bloomington, IN 47403
www.balboapress.com
1 (877) 407-4847

Because of the dynamic nature of the Internet, any web addresses or
links contained in this book may have changed since publication and
may no longer be valid. The views expressed in this work are solely those
of the author and do not necessarily reflect the views of the publisher,
and the publisher hereby disclaims any responsibility for them.

The author of this book does not dispense medical advice or prescribe the use
of any technique as a form of treatment for physical, emotional, or medical
problems without the advice of a physician, either directly or indirectly. The
intent of the author is only to offer information of a general nature to help
you in your quest for emotional and spiritual well-being. In the event you use
any of the information in this book for yourself, which is your constitutional
right, the author and the publisher assume no responsibility for your actions.

Any people depicted in stock imagery provided by Thinkstock are models,
and such images are being used for illustrative purposes only.
Certain stock imagery © Thinkstock.

Print information available on the last page.

ISBN: 978-1-5043-9551-9 (sc)
ISBN: 978-1-5043-9550-2 (hc)
ISBN: 978-1-5043-9552-6 (e)

Library of Congress Control Number: 2018900265

Balboa Press rev. date: 09/28/2018

Every Moment

Rejoice when you realize you are worrying about tomorrow.
Celebrate when you stub your toe.
Bow to the heavens when you become aware of your
Judgments and blame.
When you breathe in,
When you breathe out,
Every day,
Every hour,
Every moment:
Another opportunity to let go and clean.

Mimi Tepping

To Ram Dass,
whose light will always illuminated my path.

# Contents

## Book One

## I Love You, Clowns Are Scary

### Part One
### The Realm of Awareness

### Part Two
### The Realm of All Possibilities

## Part Three
## Beyond the Beyond

# Book Two

# Celebrating Ho'oponopono

## Part One
## The Pono Club

## Part Two
## Easy Meditations and Visualizations

## Part Three
## Many Teachers

## Part Four
## The Psychotherapeutic Connection

# *Ho'oponopono*

## "Hu - oh po - no po - no"

*H*O'O is the Hawaiian word for make, cause or bring about; it is like the word "to" in front of a verb. This book is about an easy way we have to make something good happen.

There is no word in English that defines pono exactly and it can have many meanings. Being pono in all your relationships means to be

sincere...responsible...correct...good... excellent...
fair ...caring loving...peaceful...honest...in harmony...
just...moral...necessary prosperous...virtuous...
beneficial successful...truthful...right...upright...
without negative energy...helpful...in perfect order

**Ponopono** means perfection, being right in all relations, making right even more right.

**Ho'oponopono** is an ancient Hawaiian healing and forgiveness practice that we can learn to make things right by taking full responsibility to correct our errors. We are able to do this by letting go of what isn't truly who we are, the thoughts and feelings we have held on to, whether we are aware of them or not. When we let go, we can return to the perfection and clarity we knew when we were born. The perfection, which is our true self, reminds us that we are connected to and one with everything.

# A Message from Dakota

**H**i, my name is Dakota. I don't know about you, but sometimes life can be difficult, especially when all my friends and my family and teachers have so many judgments and opinions about me. To be honest, I can be pretty quick to judge them, too, and I can be especially hard on myself.

It used to be worse.

I used to get so perplexed. I would ask myself hard questions, like, "Why are things so difficult?" and, "What do people want from me?" and "Who am I anyway?".

Then something happened to me that helped me understand life in a new way, and things got wa-a-ay easier.

What happened?

I can tell you in one word.

"Ho'oponopono."

With Ho'oponopono I have learned that "Who am I?" is the most important question I can ask myself, and that there is a very simple way to learn the answer.

But I'm getting ahead of myself a little. Here are some things about me you might want to know. I'm seventeen, so I call myself "Dakota17" in this book, as opposed to Dakota11, the kid I was 6 years ago, or Li'l D, the kid I was when I was 4.

This book is actually two books. The first book is mainly Dakota11's story - what I've remembered about what happened to me when I was eleven. In some ways, that was another kid.

I don't even know what the heck happened to me the day I turned eleven. Sometimes I think of it as the most crazy, cool, fantastical dream I've ever had. Other times I am positive it really happened.

Still at other times I think that maybe I, Dakota11, was in the right place and time and just breathed in the perfect energy to meet my guide, Auntie Pono. Maybe she took me to some other reality. Sheesh, I don't know. You tell me. For now, let's just call it my inner journey.

When I was eleven, I had an intense fear of clowns. After my journey, I returned without the fear that I had held on to for over half my life.

After the night of my eleventh birthday I was surprised to find that I didn't let my shyness get in the way of talking to other kids about my amazing journey and asking them what they thought. Could we have parts of us inside our mind that are us when we were littler? Can we solve problems in an instant? Every question led to another question. After some of the chapters in Book One, I added a bit of information I've learned. It won't hurt to skip over the Data from Dakota sections if you just want to read the next chapter.

Book Two, Celebrating Ho'oponopono, has four parts. Part One, The Pono Club, tells about a club some friends and I started in my middle school to explore Ho'oponopono (and an internet full of related things) and a cool technique we call "slo-mo-pono", which shows how Ho'oponopono can helps us let go of problems. We had a celebration at the end of our last year of middle school. I thought I knew a lot, but I learned so much more when my friends shared how they use Ho'oponopono in their lives.

You may want to read Book Two, Chapter 5: <u>The Ho'oponopono Celebration</u> first to learn how my friends and I have been able to use Ho'oponopono ourselves. Then read Book One, <u>I Love You Clowns Are Scary,</u> all about my night time adventure, which showed me one way to understand how this ancient practice works.

Part Two of Book Two will teach you easy meditations and visualizations. You may pick one and stick with it the rest of your life. Or you can try them all out and investigate others. There are so many ways to meditate. Your way is out there to be discovered.

Part Three is full of quotes from religious leaders, people whose spirituality inspired them, and independent thinkers. They talk about love, gratitude, forgiveness, responsibility, meditation, and energy - all have a lot to do with Ho'oponopono. These are not meant to be read all at one time. You might pick one quote that is meaningful to you in the morning, reflect on it in your meditation, and it in mind for the day. Part Three ends with an ancient story, The Old Man and the White Horse, which was taught by a Chinese philosopher, Lao Tzu, over twenty-five hundred years ago.

Part Four is for parents, teachers, therapists and students of psychology of any age. It explores the various ways Ho'oponopono is woven into the fabric of how we relate to one another and of various spiritual and therapeutic approaches.

If you're the type to imagine pictures when you read books, imagine them with this in mind: When I think back on my inner journey and the characters I met, Book One, I remember it like I was in a very colorful Pixar cartoon. The rest, my life since then, looks like a regular movie in my mind.

## Data from Dakota17

Ho'oponopono is simple and easy. Because it involves spirituality and psychology, there are a lot of ideas and information that relate to it.

After some of the chapters in this book, I will use this section to share some of these ideas. If these "Data" sections interrupt or confuse the story for you, just skip them for now.

An important part of the Hawaiian culture is "ohana", which means family. Ohana is not only blood-related relatives but also, friends and neighbors. In a larger sense, there is a part of us that is timeless and has no limits. All people and all of nature is ohana. We are all family and must not forget each other. Calling an older person "auntie" or "uncle" is a sign of endearment and respect. Since I met Auntie Pono, I've learned that even unrelated people are family. By the end of my story, you will see why "Auntie" fits Auntie Pono so well.

# BOOK ONE

# I LOVE YOU,
# CLOWNS ARE SCARY

## Dakota

**D**AKOTA is every girl, every boy, every kid. All of us.

The "parts" inside Dakota's mind are examples of the idea that we all have many aspects of ourselves inside. Some hold our feelings and decisions about the world from the many experiences we've had. For example, here is a decision Dakota made at four years old: Clowns are truly dangerous because they look so weird and scary.

Others parts represent roles or jobs we have in life, like son or daughter, student, artist or athlete, defender or hider. Still others represent judgments we have about ourselves or we've adopted from what others have labeled us, like "Smart", "Slow", "Lazy" or "Hyper".

It is important to accept each of our parts, though it might be very helpful to give them new jobs or different names!

**Kid Dakota or The Kid** represents the part of our subconscious mind that is curious, capable and always willing to help. We need to communicate with this part of us. The Kid is awesome.

**L'l D** represents a younger part of us inside who has been hurt or frightened in some way. We need to treat this part of us as we would any little child - gently, with care and compassion.

## Auntie Pono

**Auntie Pono** represents all the aunties and uncles who have passed on the ancient Hawaiian wisdom through the years. In Hawaiian culture, kids call older folk "auntie" or "uncle" to show respect and because they understand that they are cared about just as if they were family. In this story Auntie Pono is Dakota's guide.

## Breeze

**Breeze** represents our observing self, the spiritual part of us that just witnesses what is going on without making judgments. Our observing self lives in the present moment and doesn't feel sadness, anger or resentment. When we are in contact with this part of ourselves, we make fewer decisions based on "right" or "wrong", "good" or "bad".

Our witness helps us stay clear headed without letting our stuck feelings and thoughts muck up our mind. The more we can see things through the eyes of our observing self, the more clearly we can see the big picture.

## Imp

**Imp** represents our imagination. The imagination is like a sixth sense that creates images and ideas. Possibly the most important job of our imagination is to be able to put ourselves in someone else's place. In this way we feel empathy and compassion for others.

The imagination is a big part of how we can figure out ways to make what we do better and easier. Because our imagination has no limits, it can be both a source of real enjoyment and unnecessary pain.

Scientist tell us that our imagination is processed in the Neocortex (which is the snaky-looking part of the brain on top and is just in mammals) and the Thalamus (part of the front of the brain) where nerve impulses are received and sent on to where they need to go.

## Thynk

**Thynk** represents our thinking mind, the part of us that works to make sense of the world. Throughout history, from the great thinkers of philosophy, biology, psychology and artificial intelligence, there have been many very different ideas of what thinking is exactly.

Often, the thoughts we have come spontaneously, out of the blue and without a plan. But we can also use our thoughts consciously to achieve our goals of getting what we need or want.

**The conscious mind (uhane** in the Hawaiian language) or, in this book, the Realm of Awareness, is our normal state when we are aware of what's happening. This is where we do most of our thinking. Along with the imagination, our conscious and abstract thoughts also come from the neocortex and thalamus.

**The subconscious mind (unihipili)**, here, the Realm of All Possibilities, is not separate from the conscious mind but we can considered it to be a part of the mind that is deeper and more powerful. Some people think of our subconscious mind as a great mental sea of life, energy and power, but, so far, scientists have not been able to measure it.

Our subconscious mind holds the controls for all the natural functions of our bodies, such as our heartbeat, our digestion, our blood circulation and our ability to heal ourselves. Involuntary actions, as well, come from our subconscious.

We may consciously tell ourselves what we want but it is usually necessary for us to get help from our subconscious before we can achieve it. Our subconscious mind is always ready to take suggestions from us. This is why it is in our best interest to have thoughts that remind us that we are meant to accept ourselves just as we are in any moment. Of course, we can always make improvements. The more we practice positive thinking, the more our subconscious mind will fill us with positive feelings and we can make positive changes.

**The Superconscious Mind (Aumakua), Inner Divinity, or Higher Self** are ways to describe the part of us that has never forgotten that we are not separate from Divinity (or God or Love, etc.). In Dakota's story, this part is called Beyond the Beyond. The more we allow this part of our mind to be present in our consciousness, the easier it is to let things come and go without getting stuck. And the more we let go, the easier it is enjoy the company of our Superconscious.

The more we pay attention to the non-judgmental attitude of our observing self, the easier it is for our superconscious and conscious minds to communicate. As we grow we can begin to take complete responsibility for the negative, useless thoughts and feelings we have. We can be aware that they are there only because we have held on to them in our conscious mind.

## Who Lives Where

Our Thynk always lives in our conscious mind.

Our Imp visits our conscious mind and lives in our subconscious mind. Thanks to Imp, we and our inner children can have conversations, meeting somewhere between the conscious and subconscious parts of our mind.

Our Greater Divinity, our Inner Divinity and our Breeze live in, what is referred to in this book, our personal "Sacred Gardens", headquarters for our Superconscious Mind. These parts of us also visit our conscious and subconscious minds, especially when invited.

# *Part One*

# The Realm of Awareness

## 1. WAKING UP IN THE REALM OF AWARENESS

*I*T was my eleventh birthday and my parents surprised me with a trip to the circus. I was going to see really cool circus acts ... birds of prey, trick dogs and ponies, and acrobats. I got pink popcorn and candy apples. I was having a great time, that is, until a little car drove into the center ring and seven clowns piled out.

Don't get me wrong. I wasn't surprised to see clowns at a circus. I was in fifth grade. I'd seen circus clowns on T.V. and plenty of pictures of them, but, except for little kids on Halloween, I rarely saw them in person. On one hand, I knew these clowns were regular people with clown make-up. On the other hand, along with the strong smells of the circus and everything getting louder, those clowns completely freaked me out.

I was confused. When I looked around to see if people were running away, no one else seemed uncomfortable. Those clowns bumped into each other and the people all around me laughed. When the fat one sniffed the skinny one's flower and it squirted him in the face, everyone laughed even harder.

I sat there like a bump on a log, frozen. I stared at their ugly white faces and gross black mouths, their strange eyes and weird huge feet. With their orange hair and red noses, they didn't look human. They were dressed crazy and acted crazy.

A part of me was worried that at any minute they would run into the stands and get me. I couldn't tell anyone. People would say, "They're just regular people with clown make-up. They're not going to hurt you." I was scared, and I felt embarrassed and ashamed that I was scared. I felt like throwing up and my heart was beating a mile a minute.

To top it off, I felt so uncomfortable with those feelings that I disguised them with a dark, dark mood. For the rest of the day I was either angry or impatient with everyone for no good reason. And I didn't like myself much, either. I was more than glad when it was time to go home.

That night I got dressed for bed and brushed my teeth like a robot. The only feeling I had was relief when I flossed and finally got that stupid popcorn and candy apple pieces out from between my teeth.

Before I could count to ten, I fell asleep. Suddenly, I was hearing a conversation in my bedroom. I heard a woman's voice say, "As soon as Dakota wakes up, we'll go." I sat upright in bed, half asleep. Standing at the foot of my bed was an old woman wearing a loose, flowing dress with huge colorful flowers. She was talking to a tiny man flitting around her who wore a black tuxedo, cape and a top hat.

"I'm Auntie Pono and this fellow is your imagination."

She introduced herself, "I'm Auntie Pono, And this fellow here," she said, pointing to the little man, "is your imagination. He's that part of your mind that can see the impossible and make the unreal look real. You can call him "Imp"." Imp took off his hat and bowed with a flourish.

Auntie Pono said, "Tonight, I'm going to show you an easy way to take care of your troubles. It's called Ho'oponopono. Right now, we're in the Realm of your Awareness and here's where we begin a journey into your mind. We are going to a part of your mind that you are not aware of yet. Tonight, we are going to your Gardens, your Sacred Gardens. It's a place without beginning and without end, a place where there is only light and love. It's there that you'll meet the most wonderful person you will ever know, the True You."

I wiped the sleep from my eyes and yawned. I had to take a minute to adjust to what I was seeing and hearing.

"Auntie Pono, I have no idea what you are talking about."

When I think back, it was weird how I just accepted that Auntie Pono and Imp were in my room, but they didn't feel like intruders at all. I had a sense that I had known them forever.

"My precious Dakota, remember the circus yesterday? How do you feel about that day now?" Auntie Pono asked.

"It was fun?" I said it like it was a question, and even I didn't completely believe it. Just mentioning the circus reminded me of the clowns. My heart started beating faster and the muscles in my legs tensed up, like I might have to run at any minute.

"Fun? It doesn't sound like it," Auntie Pono said. She looked deep into my eyes. "You were having lots of fun watching the circus until something happened. Right?" I nodded. Her voice was soothing and I felt comfortable listening to her.

"Dakota, when you were four years old, you made an innocent mistake by deciding to hold on tight to some scary thoughts. Along the way to your Sacred Gardens, I'll introduce you to some wonderful parts of yourself you've never met before. When we get to the Gardens, they will help you free the little you of all that fear."

My chest started feeling really tight. I was so confused that I began to feel frustrated with Auntie Pono. You could hear it in my voice.

"Right," I said. "Like we're going to take off our shoes and crawl into my ear and into my brain with a flashlight. Like we're going to form a search team and rescue some little kid who's been hanging out there for seven years."

I folded my arms in annoyance. I was dubious.

"Oh no, you can wear your shoes if you want to." she said, her brown eyes twinkling, "And you won't need a flashlight when you're inside."

"Auntie Pono!"

"It's okay to be confused, Dakota. You'll see that, just like the universe, your mind is an endless mystery. And that's more than okay!"

My anger disappeared and I chuckled. Even though Auntie Pono was talking about serious stuff, I was also watching Imp. He jumped off her shoulder and onto her head, where he did three somersaults. That Imp had a lot of energy.

"We are going to begin this trip by going into your head, but don't let that limit your thinking. Your mind is not just in your body or brain; it is part of all that exists now, has ever existed, and will ever exist in the future." I tried to make sense of what Auntie Pono was saying but it made my head spin.

Meanwhile Imp was inching down Auntie Pono's forehead until he looked directly into her left eye. "Okay, Imp, we're going," she reassured him. To me, she said, "You have a great imagination, Dakota. So for now, let Imp help you imagine that you're floating on a cloud."

The next thing I knew, Imp flew over to me and started patting my head. I began to feel relaxed and I closed my eyes. I imagined lying safe and secure on the softest of soft clouds.

"Now you can see with your mind's eye," Auntie Pono whispered to me. "Imp is already working to help you accept that, because of your amazing mind, you can, well, go inside your mind. First stop, inside the Realm of Awareness."

## Data from Dakota17

I took a psychology class in high school last year and, because of what I was studying, I finally added two and two together. When Auntie Pono talked about my Realm of Awareness, she was talking about the conscious mind, (Uhane in Hawaiian).

Consciousness has many different definitions depending whether you're a scientist, philosopher, or psychologist. Basically, it's the normal state of being awake and aware of what's happening. This is where we do most of our thinking and get a sense of who we are in our bodies and in the world.

Our conscious mind influences how we act, feel and remember. It is in our conscious mind that we begin the Ho'oponopono process to return to our perfect selves, because we consciously choose the Ho'oponopono viewpoint.

When we are little, we only know what we have been told, or what our experiences have led us to decide about the world. As we grow, we are influenced by our parents, friends, books, the media, and more experiences.

We are especially influenced by our imagination. In some ways, our conscious mind is limited, especially compared to the subconscious. The cool thing is that since we humans can consciously use our imagination, we can be creative without limits.

Another random piece of information: if you have an intense fear of clowns, you have a phobia called 'coulrophobia'. Believe me, you are not alone!

## 2. BREEZE SETTLES THYNK DOWN

The minute Auntie Pono said the words "Realm of Awareness", I was doing the very thing that I thought was impossible ten minutes before. Imp was standing on my shoulder, pointing a flashlight into my ear. At the same time, I had shrunk to the same size as Imp. And, I wasn't wearing shoes. It was all very weird. We got on our knees and crawled into my ear, which was just the right size for the smaller me. I looked behind me to see Auntie Pono following close behind.

We were somewhere else entirely. There was no floor; we didn't need one. We weren't exactly flying and we weren't floating. We just didn't seem to need a floor.

And Imp's flashlight was gone. At first, I could hardly see anything. Slowly, our surroundings got lighter. I could see splotches of pastel pinks and blues, but I couldn't make out any shapes, except for Auntie Pono and Imp, who had not left my side since I first met them in my bedroom.

Imp made himself small enough to jump onto my shoulder. For the first of many times that night he proceeded to scratch my head. He wasn't just scratching, which felt terrific, by the way. He was activating and energizing my imagination.

Quietly and quickly, a beautiful and peaceful forest grew up around me. It reminded me of a place my family went camping once, except I could see glimpses of a rainbow colored light beyond the trees. As we walked through the forest, that curtain of light captivated me and, for a moment, the forest faded.

Auntie Pono explained, "That is just one of many curtains and doors inside your mind. Behind each one is a different area of awareness. The more you get to know your mind, the easier some barriers will be to pass and travel through." It all seems incredible now, but then, everything seemed absolutely natural.

"Every day," she continued, "you will be closer to letting go of everything that isn't your True Self. All the barriers will disappear and, for fleeting moments, you will experience being connected to everything." It is six years later and I'm still figuring that one out. It's not that I don't believe it, I do. It's just that, sheesh, I'm only human and I don't always remember how to let go of stuff or that it's even possible!

When Auntie Pono said the words, "your True Self", a nearby curtain opened and a beautiful woman, formed of the same rainbow light as the curtain, came through and danced in the air. She looked a little like Miss Lilly, my third grade teacher, only her hair was gold and her eyes sparkled like stars. She floated over to us and explained herself, "I am a messenger from a place deep inside you. I carry energy from your wisest self, your Inner Divinity." Her voice was musical and her words came out like a song, a little like a lullaby. "My job is to help you see the big picture - that giant world beyond yourself. I am your observing self, but you can call me Breeze. Nothing is too big or small for me, I'm comfortable with it all and I am happy to help you through your whole life."

"The thing about Breeze," Auntie Pono said, with a loving voice that sounded a little like Breeze, "is that she is always patient, gentle and accepting." You could hear in her voice how much Auntie Pono liked Breeze. "She doesn't get mad or sad, discouraged or flustered. She doesn't compare or worry. And she never judges you."

Breeze cooed, "Of course. I only know this moment and I only know Love. Every moment lasts only for an instant, so there is no point in living at any other moment. Accept and cherish the moment you're in."

As she spoke, I became more aware of the green forest around us and it felt like it was mine. Where there hadn't been a floor before, I was now standing on soft duff left by fallen redwood needles. It felt heavenly as I inhaled the scent of the trees and the cool fresh air.

I watched as Imp flew around Breeze. He had a sappy look on his face, like he was in love. But in an instant, Imp's expression changed back to the mischievous one I had seen earlier.

He was paying close attention to another form that appeared from behind a tall tree. Imp jumped back and forth between this new character and Auntie Pono and me. As the form got closer it became clearer and I could see a little man dressed like a formal school teacher in a suit and tie. He wore a button that read, "I ♥ Logic".

This little man stood stiffly in the clearing of the trees. Clouds floated off the top of his head, like thought bubbles in the comics. The curious thing was that every thought cloud had a different shape and a different color.

"Dakota, just as I am part of your mind, so is this fellow, your thinking self," Breeze said, introducing this very serious resident, who didn't seem to be paying much attention to us. "He nicknamed himself Thynk, like Tink, or Blink, or Wink, but not as cheery and lighthearted. Together, we make quite a team because we see the world from two viewpoints. It's important to know that we are both part of you. If you're curious, those clouds he is creating are thoughts and the colors are feelings."

Auntie Pono said, "Dakota, when you plan your day or remember to do your homework or give the right answers in a math test, you have Thynk to thank. He works with your imagination, and together they come up with great ideas and and a few uninspired ones, too.

"Imp and Thynk are the reason you have such kind and generous thoughts. Because your imagination helps you sense how other people feel, you can be a compassionate person. Imp is also very helpful when you make a mistake and need new ideas to fix the error."

"However...," said Auntie Pono. She was quiet for a moment and I listened more intently. "However," she continued, "Breeze would never say so, but Thynk isn't always a team player."

Imp was standing on Thynk's shoulder, whispering in his ear, and Thynk was nodding vigorously. "Sometimes Thynk and Imp want you to believe that it's important to compare yourself to other people." Auntie continued, "Sometimes they want you to decide whether someone is right or wrong.

"It's Thynk who judges what's happening as being good or bad. It's Thynk who tells you to worry or have expectations. It's Thynk who distracts you with pictures, words and stories when you want to concentrate at school or go to sleep. And believe me, Imp is usually encouraging him."

Auntie Pono explained, "Thynk doesn't understand how he can create suffering with so many of his thoughts. He can be much louder than Breeze and sometimes he pushes her away. No problem really, Dakota. They're both important, and it's up to you to keep them in balance. Remember though, just because Thynk thought it, it doesn't mean that is real or true."

All this time, the thought clouds that were coming off Thynk's head were getting bigger and darker. Thynk was paying more attention than I thought he was. "This is a bunch of poppycock!" he pouted. "I know what I'm talking about. I'm smart and I have a job to do."

"This is a bunch of poppycock."

Imp mimicked Thynk's stance, folding his arms as if he were also angry. Thynk was getting red in the face. Imp's face became red. Breeze floated over and blew into both of their ears.

That seemed to calm Thynk's chatter long enough for Auntie Pono to say to him, "You are important, Thynk, and you certainly work hard. However, you deserve a vacation sometimes. Thank you for slowing down, Thynk."

Auntie Pono put her hand on my shoulder and said, "Dakota, there are many ways you can help Thynk calm down. One is to relax your body, finger by finger, toe by toe. Sometimes when you are nervous you may hold your breath or take extra fast and short breaths. That makes Thynk start believing that you are actually in danger.

"Slow down your breathing and Thynk will be able to take a rest. You too, Imp. When you quiet your thoughts, Dakota, Breeze will be able to help you make wise decisions." For a moment, there were fewer clouds and they brightened in color. But just for a moment.

"Give me a little credit here, folks," Thynk said. "I work hard. I never stop. I can't be paying attention to Breeze all the time. If I weren't so busy, Dakota, you would walk into the street without looking, you wouldn't know how to draw a trapezoid, you wouldn't be able to choose between chocolate or broccoli ice cream." By this time, Thynk was yelling again. Just as fast as they became lighter, the clouds got bigger and darker.

I was beginning to feel overwhelmed by the tsunami of loud thoughts coming from Thynk. The thought clouds were getting darker and they seemed to be closing in on me. I held my breath and I could feel a knot forming in my stomach.

Breeze touched my hand, and as fast as that panicky feeling had appeared, it disappeared. I let out a loud sigh and I felt my regular breath return. This time, Thynk's thoughts didn't stop me from being in charge of my breathing.

## 3. There's No Stopping Imp

Breeze tightened her hold on my hand and we began to fly around Thynk, leaving him, Imp and Auntie Pono on the ground. It felt like second nature for me to be flying this way, but I kept a steady grip on Breeze's hand as we spiraled to the very top of a redwood tree. We landed in a nest of sticks and twigs with soft layers of leaves and moss. "Nice touch, Imp," laughed Breeze, looking down on him. Facing me, she explained, "This is an old egret nest. Enjoy." I leaned back, caught my breath, and relaxed.

From the height of the redwood tree, I looked over the edge of the nest and could see miles and miles of forest. Beyond the trees, I saw water, beyond the water, sky, and beyond the sky, limitless space. At first, I just stared, but then I started questioning: How did I get here? What is that I see beyond the sky? How can I feel so big here and so small at the same time?

Breeze read my mind. "It is not humanly possible to make sense of it all. In this moment, it is what it is. Another time you may view this experience from a different perspective. You will remember this differently and that's okay."

As if on cue, my view of the nest, the forest, and water disappeared. We were sitting on a puff of a cloud of pastel blues, pinks, greens and yellows, and all around us were similar fluffy clouds. "Wow, Imp!", Breeze said. "You are good!"

I closed my eyes and just allowed myself to feel like I was floating on a cloud, which wasn't that hard, under the circumstances. After a while, I looked down and did a double take.

Where Thynk had stood, I saw myself with a much smaller Thynk on my shoulder, jabbering at me. Thought clouds were flying off his head nonstop. I couldn't hear what Thynk was saying, but I became exhausted just listening to him all the time. I wanted to tell him to quiet down!

At first I was really nervous, then Breeze showed me a way to calm down. She whispered into my ear, "Notice...just notice. Breathe ... slowly ... and listen."

I made myself breathe as deeply as I could. I listened to the sound of the air moving in and out of my nose. I could see more of what Auntie Pono called the Realm of Awareness. As I breathed, the clouds became lighter and there was more space between them.

The scene morphed again. Imp had skillfully created a sparkling blue ocean and a pretty little island with white sand and big palm trees. Auntie Pono signaled from the island for Breeze and me to come back. We flew in a spiral back down until we landed with a fun little bounce. I was happy to be aware of my body on this perfect little island. All my senses were alive. I loved the feeing of sand on my hands and feet. The air was warm and I took long breaths.

We all sat in a circle, Auntie Pono, Breeze, Thynk and I. Even Imp started settling down and slowly wandered in and out of our little circle. That's when Breeze told me that the reason she looked the way she did was because Imp was creating her in that particular form.

"I want you to know that I'm an energy always available to you," Breeze said. "One thing I can do is help you let go and clean yourself of uncomfortable thoughts and feelings. I'm here to remind you that, although you may have thoughts or feelings, they are not who you are," Breeze said. Boy, was that confusing!

"Auntie Pono called me your observing self. Other people call my energy the breath of God. Others call me their witness or an advisor. You might want to think of me the way you see me now, but you could also imagine a dragonfly or two loving eyes and a gentle voice or whatever feels right to you. You may keep me invisible and just feel my energy.

"It doesn't really matter how you see me, Dakota. Just keep your mind open to the possibility that looking through Thynk's eyes may not be the only way to see the world."

Auntie Pono said, "Just for now, Thynk, I'd like you, Imp and Breeze to demonstrate what can happen with Dakota's thoughts."

Then she whispered something to Thynk, who started talking to himself. Imp jumped from shoulder to shoulder.

Thynk voiced all sorts of thoughts I know I'd had at different times, "It would be great not to have to go to school ever again. But how would I learn anything; I love learning. There's the internet. School's dumb. Sheesh, but I like school usually. I have some good friends. Tests suck. Aarg!"

I cracked up listening to myself. I know that Imp and Thynk were mere characters representing my imagination and my thought process, but they were perfect. Sometimes I have so many thoughts and they are all over the place. The Buddhist phrase is "monkey mind". They got that right.

"See how a thought may start out light and fluffy," said Auntie Pono, pointing to the thoughts-about-school clouds coming off Thynk. "When Thynk is sure his thoughts are the only ones possible, it's like he's holding on to the cloud. Watch how the longer he holds it, the darker and dirtier it becomes. Thynk is sure he's helping by holding on tightly. Sometimes he's sure he's protecting you, and sometimes he's convinced that it's important to make you the only one who is right."

Auntie Pono swept her fingers through the sand as she spoke, "On the other hand, Breeze looks at the situation in a whole other way. You've got to love Breeze. One of her jobs is to remind you that you can have different thoughts and emotions at one time."

"I don't get it!" I interrupted, frustrated.

"Do you ever get impatient or angry with friends or people in your family?"

"Duh!"

"Well, Breeze helps you be aware that when you're feeling angry, you still love them. If you invite her to help, Breeze can make it comfortable for you to hold more than one thought at the same time." She nodded to Breeze and said, "If you please..."

My jaw dropped as I watched Breeze become translucent and grow larger than the clouds. She scooped thought clouds coming off Thynk's head and held them like pillows against her body. When she had an armful of dirty clouds, she threw them into the sky. The air filled with sparkling lights, all the colors of the rainbow. I was flabbergasted.

"Thank you, Breeze," said Auntie Pono.

Auntie Pono whispered something to me. I turned to Thynk and repeated what she suggested I say, "And thank you, Thynk.

I'm so glad that you are a part of me. Thanks for listening to Breeze when she reminds you that you might be working too hard."

"While we are expressing our gratitude, let's take a moment to thank Imp for helping Thynk," said Auntie Pono. "Without imagination, we wouldn't have paintings or buildings or rocket ships or cookie recipes.

"Even more valuable, our imagination is how we are able to understand how other people feel. We behave in kind ways because we can imagine in our body and mind how other people might feel if we did or said something that hurt them.

"It's a gift to be able to have that much empathy. And we have Imp to thank for that." Imp hopped onto the palm of Auntie's hand, and she laughed as he started flexing his muscles in an exaggerated pose.

While Auntie Pono was helping me understand how valuable my imagination is, and Imp was providing entertaining shenanigans, Breeze transformed into a long golden ribbon. She floated around us like an angelic hug.

## Data from Dakota17

One of the happiest memories of the trip through my eleven-year old mind, is that either Breeze or the golden ribbon was always there for me, dancing in the air. Sometimes both.

Here are some of my thoughts about thoughts. Thoughts are important, but sometimes we get carried away with thinking that our thoughts are all there is. Sometimes there are things we need to pay attention to, but we let thoughts distract us. Our thoughts may be significant and creative or they may be mean or meaningless, but we are not our thoughts. Who are we then?

Six years down the road, I understand how magical it is to have an inside helper like Breeze to get through rough times. In the most gentle of ways I am reminded that I don't know everything. Occasionally, I get off my high horse and I can listen to my observing self. I will realize that I've been assuming that I know how other people feel and why they do what they do. Considering how often I take things personally, and how much better I feel when I accept what happens in my life, this feels magical!

## 4. THE TOOL BOX

For a while, no one said a word. We listened to the water lapping against the beach and basked in the warmth of the sun. Auntie Pono pulled a big red toolbox out of a tiny pocket in her dress. This seemed impossible to me until I looked at Imp, who was jumping up and down in glee, enjoying his magical creation.

Auntie Pono opened the box which held several scrolls, each rolled up and tied with a silk gold ribbon. "These scrolls," she said, "are full of tools to help us be the people we were meant to be - patient, kind, and caring." She paused, then added, "And happy!"

Auntie Pono removed the largest scroll. As she was untying its ribbon, she faced Thynk and said, "Thynk, I'm going to read something to you. It's the Ho'oponopono Choice. Dakota's life will be easier and happier when you consider making this choice for yourself." She slowly read it to Thynk but, believe me, I paid attention to every word.

## The Ho'oponopono Choice

I choose to remember that my purpose on Earth
Is to know, to be, and to express my True Self,
By valuing what is important to me and
Honoring the same worth in all beings.

My thoughts and feelings are not who I truly am.
I understand that I will always experience
Thoughts and feelings, and
I recognize that my responses to what
Happens in my life are totally up to me.
I choose to take 100% responsibility
For all that I am aware of.
I am willing to mend my errors.

I am grateful for the opportunity
To experience life in a human body,
With a loving heart and a creative mind.
I choose to express my gratitude
By remembering to clean all the time,
Letting go of thoughts and feelings
That are not my True Self.

Note from Dakota17: more on your "true self" in the Data from Dakota section that follows this chapter.

Even though he listened intently to Auntie Pono, Thynk was full of questions. "How in the world am I going to do that?" asked Thynk. "One hundred percent responsibility? What am I cleaning? Clean all the time? Give me a break! And anyway, what do you mean by tools? All I see is rolled up paper."

Auntie Pono took a deep breath which seemed to encourage Thynk to do so as well. "A tool, you see, need not be a hammer or a wrench, but can be a way for you to let go or bounce back from something difficult. It can help you wash away problem and memories stuck in your mind. Making the Ho'oponopono Choice is one tool. This will make things clearer," she said, as she unwrapped the remaining scrolls.

# A FEW CLEANING TOOLS

Focus on the "in breath" and the "out breath"

Say out loud or think to yourself...

"I'm sorry, please forgive me, thank you, I love you."
or "I love you" or "Thank you" or
"I'm sorry, please forgive me."

"Delete.", "Defragment.", "Erase."

"Thy will be done." or "Let go and let God."

Eat jelly beans

Put your attention on feelings in your body
like love, gratitude or forgiveness.

Open and close your fists or your eyes.

Drink fresh water and eat nutritious or tasty food.

Sing funny or loving songs.

Imagine stuck feelings being blown free
and floating away.

## SOME OF THE "STUFF" WE NEED
## TO CLEAN AND WHEN

Remember, there are other words for cleaning: for example, "letting go", "releasing" and "freeing". We can clean all the time...for example, when we're folding clothes, eating lunch, walking down steps, waiting for a class to begin, going to sleep or calming our temper or our fears. When we clean, we are handling the problem. What are we cleaning? We are cleaning our stuff! And do we have a lot of stuff!

assumptions...worries...drama...blame...fear...anger... needing to know what can't be known... shame...memories of the past, fantasies of the future...data...regret...illusions... stuck energy... resentments...disappointments...stuck sadness... anticipation...frustrations...making comparisons...criticizing... excitement...expectations...negative judgments about ourselves and others... memories of our ancestors, the plants, the seas and the beginning of time.

# WE CAN ALSO CLEAN
# THOUGHTS LIKE THESE:

I'm going to fail the test coming up.
I how she is going to react.
I know what he will say.
Something is wrong with me because I don't
know what I want to be when I grow up.
I'm ashamed I acted like a bully and I can't undo it.
I hate myself because I'm not good
enough to get on the soccer team.
My parents are getting a divorce...It's my fault....I
should have figured out a way to keep them together.
I'm jealous of her because she's so talented
(cute, rich, etc.).
My teacher is never fair.
My friend moved away...I'll never be happy again.
It's always my fault... She's stupid... I'm stupid

WHEN THESE THOUGHTS ARE TRANSMUTED
(TRANSFORMED) THEY BECOME PURE LOVE.

After he read and reread the last scroll, Thynk quietly rolled up all the scrolls, bowing in thanks as he handed them to Breeze, who tied each of them with a silk ribbon. Auntie Pono set them in that big red tool box, closed it and magically put it back in her tiny pocket.

Thynk furrowed his brow. "Don't worry," said Auntie Pono, laughing. "That big ol' tool box and those pieces of paper are gone, though you may find those exact words written in a book somewhere. And the information is yours to store in that amazing brain of yours, where you will, no doubt, be adding more ideas and tools during your whole life! Soon, you and Dakota will have an important helper to do much of the work. Have patience, Thynk." She smiled, knowing that having patience was sometimes Thynk's biggest challenge.

## Data from Dakota17

Ho'oponopono reminds me that we are all born with our own spark of Divinity. Divinity may be a concept you connect to a religion, but you can have no religion and have a relationship to your own divinity. You can call this part of all of us a name like "God" or "Love" or "Infinite Wisdom", depending on your personal perspective. That little piece of Divinity in all of us connects us with everyone and everything. It is our Inner Divinity that looks out from behind our eyes.

This is the True Self. Another word for True Self is Perfect Self. It is the part of us that doesn't compare or judge. It merely observes. Some people call it the Spark of Divinity.

One way I learned how to understand my True Self was to think of what a little baby looks like and remember that once I, too, was a baby. When we were born, our minds were clear. We didn't worry about the future or regret the past. We were always present in the moment. We simply were. We didn't know anything about time. It was always just "now" to us. We hadn't developed opinions about people yet or been affected by their judgments.

We are our True Self when we feel truly alive and loving. We are true to ourselves when we are calm, content and focused, alert and aware. When we learn from our experiences without judging ourselves, we stay in touch with our True Self. We are truly ourselves when we remember that we have never really been separated from Divinity.

I am grateful that I have a life of freedom to search for what is true and right for me. My understanding of my True Self, and you and your own understanding, will change often because the one thing we can count on is change.

You may have heard the quote from William Shakespeare, "This above all, to thine own self be true." A lighter quote, attributed to another writer, Oscar Wilde, is "Be yourself-everyone else is already taken." Let me know if you know who added this: "Be yourself, unless you can be a unicorn and then, always be a unicorn."

There are over three hundred words for divinity and inner divinity, including words for people who don't believe in a god, divinity or God. Following are a few:

## Just some of the words for
## "DIVINITY"

GOD, GODDESS
INFINITE PEACE... SPIRIT
UNIVERSAL FORCE
THE ALL
THE INFINITE LIGHT AND LOVE OF THE UNIVERSE
CREATOR...LOVE...THE ONE...ZERO LIMITS
UNIVERSAL CONSCIOUSNESS
DIVINE INTELLIGENCE...SOURCE... COSMOS
THE VOID...EMPTINESS...SEA OF LOVE
CREATIVE LIFE FORCE...THE GRAND EQUATION
PERFECT PEACE
DIVINE LOVE...A RIPE PEACH...RAM...THE UNIVERSE
INTERCONNECTED WEB OF ALL EXISTENCE
NOT GOOD-NOT BAD- JUST IS
ALL THAT IS...THE SOUNDS FROM A CELLO
THE GREAT BIG THING
UNIVERSAL MIND...THE FORCE
AUTHOR OF PEACE
GREAT MOTHER ... GREAT FATHER
ALL THAT IS ... INFINITE PEACE
MOTHER NATURE...NEUTRAL...LORD
THE BLANK SLATE...ETERNAL ONE
TRANSFORMING GRACE
HEALING LIGHT...PROVIDER
THE GREAT MYSTERY
SUPREME BEING... FORMLESS...ALMIGHTY
and these names...AKUA... GAIA...YAHWEH
BRAHMA...VISHNU...SHIVA
MAYA...JEHOVAH...ISIS...ALLAH...ELOHIM

Just some of the words for
**"INNER DIVINITY"**

THE DIVINE WITHIN
DIVINE CONSCIOUSNESS
INNER WISDOM
SACRED SELF...SUPERCONSCIOUS
AUMAKUA...HOLY SPIRIT
FAIRY GODMOTHER
THAT PEACEFUL FEELING
PERSONAL ANGEL...INSIDE VISION
STILL, SMALL VOICE
DIVINE INTELLIGENCE
INNER LIGHT...GUIDANCE
SPARK OF DIVINITY
HIGHER SELF
UNSEEN THERAPIST
HIGHER INTELLIGENCE
TRUTH WITHIN
SPIRIT OF LIFE
OUR UNEQUIVOCALLY PERFECT NATURE
DIVINE CONSCIOUSNESS
PURE ESSENCE
LIFE FORCE
SOURCE

## 5. THE GUARDS AT THE GATE

With no warning and no time to regret leaving the island, we were in the redwood forest again. Breeze led us along a soft dirt path. In the blink of an eye, I watched as her form changed from that of a twirling ballerina to a golden ribbon and back again.

A couple of times Breeze slowed us down to look at this or touch that. Auntie Pono reminded me that I was in my Realm of Awareness and that I had the power to make this realm larger just by becoming more aware. Breeze was helping by getting me to pay attention to what was just in front of me when I wouldn't have otherwise. We stopped and knelt down. There on the soft dirt, I got a much closer look at the forest floor.

It wasn't just a redwood forest, though I did discover that the redwood bark was soft and kind of fuzzy. The forest was home to the most delicate of pink flowers and some very slow slugs. Gazing at the moss on a log for a while, I could imagine the moss was a miniature forest.

When I crouched close to the ground, I could smell things I couldn't when I stood up. Down low, I smelled musty smells, spicy smells, and minty smells. Many of the smells I couldn't describe because they were so new to me. Gradually, I became more aware of my sense of hearing. From a distance, I could hear moving water, from above I heard different bird calls, and, somewhere close to me but out of sight, was some sort of chirping insect.

For the first time since I met Thynk, he looked happy. He took off his tie and stuffed it into his pocket. Even though his eyes were wide open, it was like a part of him was asleep. It didn't seem strange then, but when I think about it now, it was weird. He was a little like a zombie, without the fear factor. Thynk is mostly a consciousness dweller, and I now know that he was acting oddly because we were getting close to a very different place in my mind.

We continued on, gliding slowly down a dirt path. The path stopped at a pretty little park, with comfy looking benches scattered here and there. Ignoring the benches, Auntie Pono motioned us to a small hill, where I gratefully sprawled out on the lush grass and closed my eyes.

The scent of the warm air filled my nostrils and I petted the soft blades of grass beneath me. Sometimes all I noticed was my breathing, and sometimes I was focused on the conversations of birds. I felt so much peace inside.

Auntie Pono gave me what seemed like enough time to rest, but I couldn't tell you if it was twenty minutes or two seconds. She pulled me up into a sitting position and said, "I want Thynk and you to play a game I call "The limits of relying on thought".

I opened my eyes and stretched. As I got my bearings, she continued. "Thynk," she said. "Be aware of how old Dakota is." Two long clouds shaped like the number one came off the top of Thynk's head. "Good, now how do you spell cat?" The cloud letters 'C-A-T' drifted above him. "Now, describe the sensation Dakota feels touching the grass." The word "S-O-F-T" appeared in the form of a cloud that floated over Thynk's head.

"Good job, Thynk. Here's a question for you. When you thought of the word that described the sensation of Dakota's fingers touching the grass, were you thinking of Dakota's age?" Thynk slowly shook his head. "Now that you are thinking about Dakota's age, are you aware of the sensation of Dakota's fingers?" Thynk shook his head again, looking a little puzzled.

"Try this, Thynk. Don't think of a pink, polka-dotted elephant." Even serious Thynk got a good laugh to see that he was creating a parade of pink polka-dotted elephant-shaped clouds. He looked at me with a coy smile, as if to say, "Well, maybe I'm not as much in charge of my thoughts as I thought I was."

Auntie Pono was satisfied. "Onward," she said, leading us around the hill we'd rested on. The path we were on led us to a sparkling blue-green stream. I peered down and saw what looked like tiny balloons of light bobbing downstream. Some were a glistening gold while others were a murky brown, and there was everything in between. A few were clear and others were like mirrors. Some seemed smooth and others bumpy. Some seemed to vibrate and others spun while they floated along.

My eyes followed the river and suddenly I was seeing something that took my breath away and stopped me in my tracks. All my attention was focused on what was in front of us.

It was the coolest bridge ever, made of interlocking bricks of glass. Each brick was cut like a diamond with many sides. When the sun hit the bricks, flashes of soft rainbow light shone on the ground and plants around us.

Just as I was getting used to the beautiful light all around me, I spotted rainbow curtains at each end of the bridge. They went up and up forever. I know forever is a long way, but I bent way back trying to see the top of these curtains. Not possible. They just kept going up!

A sign in front of the bridge with an arrow pointing to it read, "To the Realm of All Possibilities". Nearby, pointing back to where we had just been, was another sign that read "To the

Realm of Awareness". Just beyond the signs and right in front of the bridge was a heavy-looking gate. I was delighted to see that it was made of smaller prisms, also reflecting rainbow lights.

Suddenly, as if my view were made of cloth, a slit appeared in the fabric of space and two replicas of Thynk slipped through, as if they had been in front of me the whole time. They were at least twice Thynk's size and wore very official-looking uniforms.

The one closest to us had a big fishing net and immediately went to work. Diligently examining the stream, he scooped out some of the tiny balloons of light that were leaving the Realm of Awareness. Occasionally, the guard would throw them back in, but mostly he threw them on the ground, where they turned into a pile of dust. I was mesmerized.

The guard who seemed to be in charge of the gate to the Realm of All Possibilities was even busier than the one guarding the gate to the Realm of Awareness. Fluffy balls of light floated in streams of air toward us from The Realm of All Possibilities on the other side of the bridge. Most would bounce back when they hit the gate. From time to time one would float free of the gate and the guard would lob it back with a huge tennis racket. Less often, one would get past him and continue its journey into the Realm of Awareness.

Some of those fluffy balls of light that got past the guard floated over to me. They didn't touch me exactly; it was more like they became me. One hovered in front of me. It seemed to be inviting me to gaze into it and all I could do was stare.

I saw a universe as if it were turned inside out. I saw the swirls of galaxies and small villages in the country side. I saw hurricanes and rainbows. I saw universities and the dark side of planets. Mostly, I saw light. What I'm trying to say is: it seemed that I saw, for a moment in my life, everything. Because maybe, for that moment, I was everything. Then, poof. That puff of fluffy light was gone.

That was the only time I ever had an experience like that. I keep it close to me still because it reminds me that the Realm of All Possibilities is infinite. My attention returned to the guards in front of us.

"What's going on?" I asked Auntie Pono.

"These are the guards you have installed in your mind," said Auntie Pono.

"I don't think so," I challenged.

"Well, I don't know who else could have. Most people install their own emotional guards. Let me explain."

She pointed to the one guarding the Realm of Awareness, scooping stuff with the net and tossing it onto the ground. "He is making sure certain negative thoughts and attitudes do not go beyond the bridge into the Realm of All Possibilities," she explained. "You've been benefiting from his services since you first started thinking about right and wrong. As you grow older and become sharper, you will give him wiser and wiser instructions."

Auntie Pono gave me a little time to digest what she had said. Then she turned toward the guard batting the puffs of light back into the Realm of All Possibilities.

"You know we are all connected to each other and everything through the energy of love. Another way to say that is that we are all one. We always have been and we always will be.

That energy of love and healing from deep within us is always available.

"Now, here is our mistake, and, Thynk, I especially want you to listen to this." Thynk looked like he was struggling to keep his eyes open, but he cupped his ears to let us know he was listening intently and not falling asleep.

"We forget that we are all one," continued Auntie Pono, "and we separate ourselves from the great wisdom and healing available in the Realm of All Possibilities. We convince ourselves that we can't have any of that great power and infinite love, so we block it from coming to us.

"Aware of it or not, Thynk, you and this guard have been a team. He's only doing what you and Dakota have ordered him to do. That's the good news. With every positive choice you make, you give your guard instructions to open the gate to the Realm of Awareness just a little more."

For several moments, Thynk seemed oblivious to anyone else. With his eyes tightly closed, he held his chin in his right hand and scratched his head with the left.

Thynk slowly opened his eyes and looked quizzically at Auntie Pono. "Don't worry, Thynk," she assured him. "You have a lifetime to give your guard new orders to open the gates wider to bring in more love and wisdom." That was enough for Thynk to close his eyes once again.

Auntie Pono turned toward me and completely changed the subject. "Don't forget, you have an important reason to explore your mind. When we are deeper inside, we will be able to rescue a scared and confused little Dakota who is trembling as we speak."

She spoke quietly, but the words echoed in my head as if they had been yelled in my ears. Things didn't quite make sense to me. Even still, I totally trusted that whatever was going to happen would be okay. In the years since that time, I've thought about trust and faith and I'm still not positive what I believe. One thing I've noticed though, when I choose to have faith that I will be okay, it's easier to breathe and I take deeper breaths.

Auntie Pono was quiet for a few moments. With a reassuring voice, she continued. "Ho'oponopono reminds us to have faith and that we don't ever need to know everything. It reminds us that, as smart as we may be, as industrious and well-meaning as your Thynk is, we never have all the answers. In a little while we'll go beyond your Realm of Awareness. You will get glimpses of the Infinite Field and your Sacred Gardens, where you'll be able to peek at what is beyond."

Putting her hand on my shoulder, Auntie Pono could tell that I was getting dizzy just trying to get a mental picture of what she was talking about. Her touch steadied me. I glanced at Imp. He was scratching his head and looked pretty frustrated.

"In the future, Dakota, you'll be able to make this trip in an instant, completely on your own. Thynk won't have to come up with a bunch of ideas to explain what is exactly happening. That would be silly and impossible and would be a waste of time. The only thing you need to know now, my dear Dakota, is this: now you have an easy way to bring yourself closer to love and forgiveness, closer to your True Self."

I still felt dizzy and I had to interrupted her. "Auntie Pono, how can I do anything else if I'm making this Ho'oponopono trip all day long. That hardly sounds easy or even possible at all!"

"You'll see," she said, smiling. "When you practice forgiving yourself and the people around you, and when you let love and gratitude be with you all the time, you will notice that you have begun letting go automatically. You may also notice that you are coming up with even more creative and inspired ideas. A lot is dependent on how Thynk decides to instruct the guards at the gate." Auntie Pono turned to Thynk and said, reassuringly, "Don't decide now. Just notice. You'll see."

With that suggestion, Thynk faced both of his guards and smiled. Ever so slightly, both guards seemed to relax. With that, I relaxed a little bit, too. As I did, the streams, the bridge, and the plants, all became even more clear and colorful.

### Data from Dakota17

You know when you are half in and half out of sleep? That feeling suddenly overcame me. I was full of energy, excited to be in front of a beautiful bridge with rainbow lights all around me. At the same time, I was sitting up in my bed, in front of a bookcase and next to a window that looked out at a moonlit oak tree. I had no energy and all I wanted to do was sleep. Everything about my bedroom disappeared when I closed my eyes and flopped back down on my pillow. In no time at all, my energy and the rainbow lights returned.

I consider myself to be very lucky, because I was fully aware of a place that is supposed to be out of my awareness. What Auntie Pono called my Realm of All Possibilities, I now know to be my subconscious mind. I was moving back and forth between it and my Realm of Awareness, my conscious mind.

Our subconscious is where we store information that we may not completely understand or be aware of. All the natural functions of our bodies - our heartbeat, our digestion, our blood circulation and our ability to heal ourselves - are in the subconscious mind. Blinking and sneezing and yawning all come from the subconscious.

Our subconscious mind is not only in our brains, but exists in every cell of our bodies. This means that our subconscious holds memories throughout our body. We have memories of this morning, memories of last year, and, believe it or not, memories of the day we were born and from before we were born. The energy of all the important people in our lives, as well as our ancestors, is in our subconscious.

In a way, everything in the mind is connected. There are no separations. There is information about all of existence from the very beginning. Auntie Pono calls the whole thing "the mind", which I think makes sense.

Sometimes I don't realize how much I base my feelings on memories of the past. Even when I worry about the future, a part of me is in the past. Ho'oponopono helps me notice that when I'm having a difficult time with uncomfortable feelings, I'm probably "replaying" memories.

Just last week, someone borrowed a book I've had since I was little. Later, a sudden thought came to me that I would never see that book again. My throat tightened and my shoulders felt heavy. I felt scared and sad.

Suddenly I remembered the moment when I was five years old, in my car seat, and I realized my dad had driven off with Blue Bear on the roof of the car. Blue Bear was my royal blue teddy bear who was my best friend. My dad went back and looked for him, but never could find him. Even though my heart was broken and I was so little, I feel good now remembering that I forgave my dad right there and then!

When I realized how devastated I had been, I wanted to comfort the five-year old I was then. I "cleaned" by imagining giving a fuzzy blue blanket of warm wishes to this younger me, who must have felt that love because I started to feel less sad about the book that had been borrowed, less scared and lonely, and lots happier.

# *Part Two*

# The Realm of All Possibilities

## 6. DAKOTA MEETS THE KID, LI'L D AND CLOWNS ARE SCARY

*I*t was time to leave the realm we had meandered through. Auntie Pono led us through an opening in the gate. All of us - Breeze, Thynk, Imp and I - glided along the bridge between the realms of my mind. Stopping in the middle of the bridge, I could see everything from a different perspective. I saw so many little streams below that I couldn't count them. From above, they looked like they were filled with millions of tiny lights. They were going both ways - into and out of the Realm of Awareness and the Realm of all Possibilities.

"Some of those lights are pieces of information from the deepest part of your mind." said Auntie Pono. "They will be formed as thoughts when they get to Thynk in the Realm of Awareness. Some will be very clear to Thynk and you will be able to use them. Some will be almost invisible and may silently slip away. Before now, Thynk assumed his job was to instruct one of the guards to hold tightly to certain uncomfortable thoughts. Soon, you will know more about cleaning and letting go and you'll be able to help Thynk get rid of troublesome thoughts more easily."

I was still confused. I decided to let go of needing to know everything and to trust that Auntie Pono would help me understand. I asked her about the streams going into the deeper realms. "Those bits below are pieces of information that have been coming to you since before you were born until this moment. That's enough for you to know today."

I looked back and could see one of the guards industriously throwing pieces of stuff away from the stream and onto the ground, where they fizzled and rapidly evaporated. The other guard was just as busy batting puffs of light away from the Realm of Awareness.

We walked to the end of the bridge and through the towering rainbow curtain. Breeze, now in her gold ribbon form, wafted over our heads like a pet bird. At first, all I could see, besides the curtains and the ribbon, was darkness, and all I could hear was a low hum. Then I felt Imp scratching my head. From that time on, I could see what was in front of me with, as Auntie Pono called it, my mind's eye.

What I saw was unlike anything I could have imagined before. I was in a huge dome with walls of constantly changing rainbow lights. Like before, there was no floor. In this place, treading air was as natural as walking.

"Remember, Thynk and Dakota, when I said you would have an important helper?" asked Auntie Pono. She pointed to the center of the dome. "I want to introduce you to Kid Dakota, also known as The Kid."

Sitting at a desk with a sign that said "Info Central" was a smiling me, looking very kind and confident, my age or maybe just a little older. On The Kid's wrist was a huge watch.

Auntie Pono explained that the watch was a computer and that The Kid could retrieve as much information as any human about what's going on in my subconscious mind.

"The clearer you are with instructions to Kid Dakota, the more efficiently the computer will work," she said. I was mesmerized staring at Kid Dakota's watch.

"Yep, InnerMindMap™ is my preferred browser," Kid Dakota explained. "It gives me access to many parts of our mind. I'm just the data manager for the computer and I can only access a small part of what's in the deeper realms.

"Right, Dakota," Auntie Pono gently interrupted, "your inner computer goes way beyond what Kid Dakota's watch can access. It's keeping your heart beating and your blood flowing and your food digesting. It has a file on everything that's ever happened to you. It is mostly on automatic and works constantly."

Kid Dakota stood up and I noticed, for the first time, this other 'me' was wearing a huge bulging backpack. I felt a little heavy just looking at The Kid with that hefty pack.

I let go of that thought when Kid Dakota spoke to me. It was as if we'd known each other our whole lives. "I understand that I'm here to help you connect to places in the Realm of All Possibilities and I'm always happy to be at your service." With wide open arms, The Kid added, "I'm always available. By that, I mean I never, ever sleep."

I was already beginning to like this take-charge part of me a whole lot.

"Auntie Pono's filled me in a bit. Here's how I might be able to help. Say you decide to make the Ho'oponopono Choice," The Kid began explaining. "Say you want to keep cleaning and letting go even when you're asleep. Just show me during the day or remind me right before you go to sleep that you want me to clean. I'll take over and get the job done when you fall asleep, or even when you get distracted during the day."

Now I was beginning to understand how "I" could let go of negative thoughts all day and still do regular things. Even though I had seen the scrolls in the red toolbox. I needed more information. "Auntie Pono," I asked, "Why am I cleaning? And what am I cleaning with? And how do I do it?"

"Imp can help you understand this," said Auntie Pono, laughing quietly as Imp flew into action, flitting around my head like a hummingbird. "Think of your One True Self as a light bulb shining with the same light as the sun above it. It can shine a light on every problem and help you come up with answers, the next step, or simply the patience to wait."

Over Thynk's head, an image of a light bulb with a floating miniature sun over it appeared. As Auntie Pono spoke, Imp flitted about, dramatically pointing to the light bulb.

"Your True Self is not only connected to something we can call Divinity, but it's also a part of it." "Some people call Divinity "God" and some call it "Love". Some call it "Mother Nature" and some call it "The Great Big Thing".

Imp pointed excitedly to the image of the sun.

Auntie Pono directed a big smile to Imp and continued. "Sometimes you let Thynk hold on to worries or judgments or resentments or decisions that are't helpful to you anymore. When you do, it's like a moth flying toward the light bulb and getting stuck on it."

I watched as, one by one, little flying bugs came from the dark toward the light bulb over Thynk's head. One by one they got stuck on the bulb.

Auntie Pono continued, "After a while, it can look more like just a bunch of gunk and it will give out less and less light. You've let negative thoughts stay stuck to memories. Your True Self is still there, but the light isn't getting through. Inside, you may be having trouble feeling the Light of Divinity.

"Please, Thynk," said Auntie Pono, calling him over to her. She whispered to Imp, who took his hat off and held it in front of Thynk.

"Inside this hat," she said to Thynk, "there are words you can use as cleaning tools. Some are quite lovely, but you could make up a completely new one tomorrow, as long as it can remind you how freeing it is to let go of worries, to choose not to stay mad or believe old beliefs you've had for years. It would be just as magical."

With that, Thynk closed his eyes and pulled out a card. "'I Love You'," announced Auntie Pono, reading the card to Dakota. "So be it. For today, your cleaning tool is 'I Love You'. As we explore, whenever you think of it or Breeze reminds you, allow the words 'I Love You' to come to you. If you have impatient thoughts: 'I Love You'. When you notice your chest is tight and you are feeling afraid: 'I Love You'. When you realize you have already decided what the future will bring: 'I Love You'. When you feel grateful: 'I Love You'.

"Who am I saying it to?" I asked, somewhat frustrated.

"Good question," Auntie Pono answered. "You can direct it, aloud or to your mind, to someone you love, your mom or your cat. You can say it to your house, the hills behind your house or your science fair project. You can say it to your Inner Divinity or The Divine. You can say it to Love itself. You can say it to the energy you disturbed with your negative thoughts.

"You can direct it to people you don't know, but who need love. Sometimes the person who needs to hear it the most is yourself. You can say it to a younger part of yourself or to a part of your body that is in pain. You can always just say or think it without attaching meaning to it. It will get to where it is needed."

What a relief it was to hear I don't have to know exactly what's happening, who or what to say "I love you" to. I could tell Thynk was also feeling more comfortable with this new idea, Ho'oponopono. Thynk got more and more relaxed and heart bubbles floated over his head. One by one, the moths, an irridescent light reflecting off their wings, flew off the light bulb.

Breeze, taking the form of a dancer again, twirled over to Thynk. Imp created a scale like the one that the statue of Lady Justice holds. Breeze slid down inside the bowl on one side, lying on it as if it were a hammock. Guided gently by Auntie Pono, Thynk climbed into the bowl on the other side, where he sat cross-legged and cross-armed. The two were perfectly balanced.

For the moment, I felt perfectly balanced, too. I could trust my thoughts not to overwhelm me and I could trust my intuition. I definitely was paying attention to what was happening, but I wasn't making up stories about the past or the future. Anything could happen today and I knew I would be okay.

"Kid," said Auntie Pono, "we're ready for you to help us find Dakota's very frightened Four-Year-Old Self." The Kid smiled and focused on the watch. While we waited for The Kid to get the needed information via the InnerMindMap™ app, something cool happened. My mind went right to the "I Love You" cleaning tool and the thought came to me: *So this is choosing.*

Sooner than I expected, Kid Dakota pointed to a table in a dark corner a little ways away. Under the table, curled up in a little ball, was a small child holding tightly onto something I couldn't see. Trembling sobs broke the silence.

I had no idea what to do.

When I looked at Auntie Pono for help, all she did was smile and nod. The Kid and I got closer and I sat down, cross-legged, close but not touching-close. Auntie Pono whispered words for me to repeat, "Hello, Little One. I'm you, but eleven years old. Please may I sit with you?" The terrified child nodded slowly. "I'd like to call you Li'l D. Is that okay with you?"

The answer to this question was a tiny, shy smile. I was kind of nervous to say anything, because I didn't want to make matters worse.

"Please, come out," I finally whispered. "I can see I...uh, you...I mean, you have been scared for a long time, but you're safe. You're not alone. You don't have to worry anymore. You don't have to be scared."

It took forever, but finally Li'l D cautiously crawled into my lap.

"Please, come out," I finally whispered.

We sat together quietly for a long time. I asked for permission to touch Li'l D, received it in the form of small nod, and gently stroked the quivering child's head and shoulders. After a while I could feel both of us relaxing. That's when I saw what Li'l D was holding on to so tightly.

At first it looked like a sweet, raggedy, cloth clown doll. Then I realized it had a scary-looking face with a mouth full of sharp teeth. I was even scared.

"Who's that and why are you holding on to it so tightly?" I asked.

"His real name is 'Clowns Are Always Dangerous', but I call him 'Clowns Are Scary', and sometimes I just call him 'Scary,

Scary'", Li'l D said seriously. "Look how scary he is. He protects me because he reminds me that I need to stay afraid so I don't get close to any clowns. All clowns are very dangerous."

Soft heart clouds started sprouting out of Thynk's head and circled around us. In that moment we both understood that Li'l D was just expressing the thoughts I had when I was four. I reached toward the clown doll and asked, "Li'l D, can I hold Clowns Are Scary for a minute?"

Immediately, that very small young me responded with a blood curdling scream that scared the heck out of the eleven year old me. I immediately backed off. Auntie Pono whispered more words in my ear for me to say to my little four-year old self.

"My dear Li'l D," I said, moving just a little closer, "for a real long time you've been holding on to the idea that clowns are always dangerous. I'm sorry I didn't tell you earlier that that thought was a mistake." Li'l D stared at me with wide eyes as I continued.

"Please forgive me for only now telling you that you are a totally awesome kid and you are not alone. Thank you for being in my life, for helping me and letting me help you. I love you and we are going to fix that mistake."

We sat quietly together until I said, "Scary, Scary doesn't look very happy. Would you like to come with us so we could help him feel better?" Li'l D nodded shyly.

We all moved away from the table and stood under a tree that Imp had created for us. Auntie Pono told Li'l D and me to each hold a hand of the Clowns Are Scary doll. It took a little while, but Li'l D let go of one of the doll's hands so I could hold it. I took it and held on to one of Li'l D's hands. Auntie Pono suggested we look into Scary, Scary's eyes and asked that I repeat her words.

"Clowns Are Scary," I said, following Auntie Pono's instructions. "I am so sorry that I've kept you stuck in my mind for so long. Please forgive me for not releasing you sooner." That little clown rag doll actually seemed to be listening. "Thank you for trying to protect Li'l D all this time, and we have learned even better ways to keep Li'l D safe. I love you. Clowns Are Scary, and I'm going to help set you free."

## Data from Dakota17

Back when I was eleven, it felt good to say all this, but I couldn't imagine how I was going to set Clowns Are Scary free. Now I understand that it was because I was taking responsibility for the problem and was willing to correct it. It was because I was willing to let go of thoughts and allow another part of me (beside Thynk) to be in charge.

Before we got to the Realm of All Possibilities, Auntie Pono said that when we got there I'd begin to get an idea of what is inside, but just an idea. She said that I wouldn't want to be aware of everything; otherwise I'd have so many pictures and sounds and pieces of information running through my mind that I'd go bonkers.

That was some very solid advice.

Ho'oponopono reminds us that we hold all the memories our soul has collected through eternity, even the small things that may seem to have nothing to do with us. The subconscious is not really separate from the conscious mind, but we can consider it to be a part of the mind that is deeper and more powerful. It is also known as the unconscious, the deep mind or the dreaming mind.

Although we may consciously tell ourselves what we want, it's necessary for us to get help from our subconscious before we can achieve it. And here's the cool part. Our subconscious mind is not only in our head, but exists in every cell of our body.

Our memories are always active, even when we're not consciously aware of them. Our memories and experiences have created our beliefs and habits and actions. Sometimes, just because we're human beings, we respond to people or situations automatically. That's "acting out of habit".

I don't know about you, but sometimes I, Dakota17, say things or do things out of habit without thinking about what I'm doing first. This sometimes makes my life difficult. Since I've made the Ho'oponopono Choice, I notice more often when I've spoken or acted without thinking. I'm more likely now to forgive myself and, at the same time, remind myself that I'm still one hundred percent responsible for my behavior.

## 7. THE IMAGINATION FACTORY

After sitting for a while with Li'l D and Clowns Are Scary, Auntie Pono give the nod for Kid Dakota to begin our cerebral tour, an exploration into my mind. She beamed when she announced to us that, with a few sightseeing detours, The Kid would be leading us to a special place deep within the Realm of All Possibilities - my personal Sacred Gardens.

"I generally don't go very far into the deeper realms, so thank you, Auntie Pono, for asking me to help. I'm excited to see how sophisticated the mapping function is on InnerMindMap™, and maybe learn a few things about rewiring Dakota's brain.

By the way, Thynk," said a smiling Kid Dakota, tapping the watch, "this internal computer is way smarter than any computer that humans have built. So, don't presume you can out think it."

Thynk looked up to see Breeze, in her golden ribbon form, circling above him. He snatched the ribbon and draped it elegantly over his neck.

Thoughtfully, Thynk said, "Both kinds of computers are smart, but Dakota's tablet at home can't store or organize information anywhere near to what that cool watch you have on can do. In Dakota's mind I trust."

The moment Thynk started talking about this decision to let go of needing-to-know-everything, a ray of light came from far in the distance and shone directly on him, like a bright spotlight.

"Hey, I just had an idea," he said, oblivious to what had just happened. "I think Imp should create a protective suit for me and the Dakotas. There is so much going on in the deeper realms that I, for one, would feel overwhelmed if I heard and saw and felt everything there. While you're at it, Imp, make us a rope so none of us floats off, Okay?"

"Inspired!" said Auntie Pono, recognizing that when Thynk let go of needing to have all the information, the Light of Inspiration (Love, Divinity, etc.) shone on him. That was how he got the notion to protect everyone from the overwhelming sights and sounds of the Realm of All Possibilities.

No sooner than you could say, "Imp, please and thank you," I, Auntie Pono, Li'l D, Kid Dakota and Thynk were all outfitted with dark glasses, ear plugs, and a suit made of tiny mirrors. Thank you, Imp, for being so creative and thank you, Thynk, for the letting go!

We made quite a parade. Imp created a translucent rope for everyone to hold on to so no one would get lost. Kid Dakota, keeping an eye on the watch, led the way. Imp sat on my shoulder while I held Li'l D's hand, who held on tightly to Clowns Are Scary. Thynk and Auntie Pono held the rope behind me, and Breeze floated above.

This exploration party was ready!

We started from Info Central, Kid Dakota's desk in the open area of the dome. Toward the outskirts of the dome were closed offices, most with a sign on the door. Like the curtain at the end of the bridge to the Realm of All Possibilities, the walls of the offices rose to a height beyond what I could see.

Auntie Pono stopped us in front of a plain-looking door with a small sign that said, "DAKOTA'S IMAGINATION FACTORY - FRONT OFFICE". With a flourish, Imp produced a wand from inside his top hat and pointed it at the door. He put the wand back into his hat, the door slowly opened, and he bounced on in. To my surprise, we walked into an absolutely white room that was empty except for a certificate on the wall.

Imp right away created a pail full of sticks of colored chalk and handed it to Li'l D, who scribbled on the walls nonstop until it was time to leave. Even though I didn't recognize anything Li'l drew, it looked beautiful.

Thynk got up close to read the certificate. He read it several times, each time turning around to look at Imp again. He was stunned. Imp, scribbling with Li'l D, was totally oblivious of Thynk's sudden adoration. I wasn't quite that stunned, but I was impressed. So cool to realize what a gift my imagination is.

The certificate itself was pretty entertaining - every so often, it changed font, all the while keeping its glittery gold colored ink. First, it was like the font you're reading (Bodini, it's called). The letters became cursive; next, all big capital letters; finally they stayed still when they became something like the font (called Papyrus) you will see on the next page.

The Union of
Body, Mind and Soul
Hereby Awards this Certificate of Appreciation to

# Dakota's Imagination

In Recognition of Talent for
Creating New and Unique Images
Solely by
Combining what Dakota
Has Seen, Heard or Felt before.

Gratitude is given for contributions
in these and other areas:
Story Telling, Making Sense of the World,
Dreaming, Pretending, Memory,
Helping Dakota's Body Heal,
Figuring Out Math and Friendships, Enjoying Books,
Drawing, Music and Dance,
Learning New Skills, Teaching Others,
Making Plans, Building and Fixing Things,
Having an Open Mind for Different Ideas
and, Especially, for Teaching Dakota
Compassion.

Signed, THE GREAT BIG THING
AKA: GODDESS, GOD, LOVE, etc.

Imp pulled a computer out of nowhere and brought up a map of the factory. The Kid tapped the watch's InnerMindMap™ app, synching Imp's map to the watch's data bank. Maybe Kid Dakota understood it, but the map was so complicated that it was beyond me to make sense of it at all.

Auntie Pono asked The Kid and Breeze to keep watch over Li'l D, so she and Imp could show me and Thynk at least one department in the factory before we left. How Imp decided which department was almost as interesting as what I found when we got there.

Imp stood absolutely still with his eyes closed. He stretched his left hand out and, from out of the blue, a white tennis ball fell into it. With his eyes still closed, he tossed the ball up and two balls came down, one into each hand. He tossed those up and four came down. Thynk, enjoying the challenge of keeping track, announced the amount of each new set of tennis balls. Imp repeated the doubling process until he was juggling sixty-four balls. Then, as fast as they appeared, they disappeared - except one ball. Imp opened his eyes and read what was written. Delighted, he showed me the ball. In large print, were the words "Dream Kitchen".

Imp threw the ball against the white wall a few times and a section of the wall became a rainbow-colored door. The door opened slowly, we entered, and on the other side was a character who reminded me of Imp and Breeze blended together.

I cannot tell you if he/she was a man or a woman, so I will refer to him/her as "they". They wore a long, flowing white robe and glided gracefully along the floor. They could have been eighteen (they had such a youthful face), or eighty (they seemed very, very wise).

With great respect in her voice, Auntie Pono introduced me, saying, "This is your Dream Maker, Dakota." Like a ventriloquist, words came out of their mouth without them moving their lips.

"Welcome to your Dream Kitchen," they said. "Good to see you, Thynk. I was just concocting a dream to serve you later, Dakota.

"First off, I need to give credit where credit is due. From the bottom of my heart, the outskirts of my mind and the center of my stomach, thank you, Imp. Without the gift of Imagination, nothing would get done in here." Thynk nodded nonstop, but Imp seemed not to be paying any attention to these words of praise as he flitted lightly from me to Auntie Pono to the Dream Maker to Thynk and back to me.

They, the Dream Maker, seemed to pick up a spoon and stir the pot enthusiastically. I'm guessing, because I really couldn't see anything in their hand. That's when I noticed some brightly-colored cauldrons bubbling wildly, just behind the dream maker.

"These bubbling pots here are full of pieces of memories and information and images," they said. "I'm letting some hard and sticky memories evaporate in this simmering one here. When the time is right I will take a scoop of this and a pinch of that and a handful of this other one, and mix them into a little story for you."

Try as I might, I couldn't identify anything in the pot. The best I can explain is that the ingredients reminded me of the little pieces of light flowing back and forth under the bridge between the Realms of Awareness and All Possibilities.

"Some of the ingredients," continued the Dream Maker, "come from information that one of the guards at your gate allows in from your daily life. Some are daily deliveries from the depths of the Realm of All Possibilities." The Dream Maker paused a moment.

"I must admit something and ask your forgiveness," they said. "Sometimes my stories come out a little scrambled and confusing. I pick the actors in your dreams from all the faces you've ever seen, including even minor characters in books and movies and people you may have just noticed as you were walking down the street. I'll tell you true, Dakota. The best stories come when I get inspiration and instructions from your Inner Wisdom, directly from your Sacred Gardens."

The Dream Maker looked at me and our eyes locked. "Dakota, life can often be lovely and sometimes it can be challenging and confusing and even painful. Sometimes I like to create dreams that help make sense of the world or fix a problem you might have.

"For example, your body knows many ways to mend and heal itself. I know those parts of yourself as your Inner Doctors. I work with your Inner Doctors to make dreams that help fix problems in your body before you know they're problems.

"You aren't supposed to remember or understand all the dreams I create, but there are some special ones I make with symbols and clues for you and Imp and Thynk to figure out. Much of the time," continued the Dream Maker, "I'm helping clean out stuff from deep storage where it isn't doing you any good.

"Which reminds me," they said. "I have a copy of a dream here that Li'l D had seven whole times in one year. In other words, it was a dream I created with what you gave me when you were much younger. Auntie Pono, here, thinks that watching it will help you understand your sweet Li'l D a bit more."

With that, the Dream Maker picked up a round laptop, opened it and entered several dates. At first, all I saw was blue sky on the screen. From somewhere in that sky, I heard a menacing cackle and saw a huge hot air balloon shaped like a clown. My heart was racing. The Dream Maker paused the video and checked in with me.

I was definitely freaked.

Auntie Pono reminded me that it wasn't real, and Breeze touched my shoulder. I assured her that I was okay and the Dream Maker continued playing the dream.

The balloon floated down to a sandy beach, not far from where I stood watching it. A giant clown, as scary as I could imagine, climbed out of the basket connected to the balloon and walked toward me.

In the dream, I ran and ran. I couldn't see where I was. All I could see were images of the balloon and the gigantic growling clown behind me, gaining on me, getting closer and closer. It felt like I was running in mud and I could hardly move, which made everything even scarier. I could feel my heart pounding wildly. Suddenly the screen turned black.

"That," said the Dream Maker, "is where you would wake up every time."

The dream seemed familiar. I thought about how scary it would be to a little kid.

"This may not make sense now, but maybe later," they continued. "The more you take one hundred percent responsibility in your life, the more clearly you will see that you can look at every part of your dreams as a part of you. Even your monsters."

Now, six years later, I, Dakota17, can see that the clown was not the monster. The monster was the fear I had attached to clowns when I was four. Li'l D (and Imp and Thynk) gave the ingredients to my Dream Maker to create the monster. When I, Dakota11, saw the clown on that round computer tablet, I felt like I was looking him right in the eyes. For the first time in my life, I knew how good it felt to face my fears head on.

"The more you are loving to every part of yourself, the more peaceful your life will be," said the Dream Maker, leading us to the door. "My best advice: Don't take anything too seriously, including Ho'oponopono. Pleasant dreams!"

"Whoa," said Auntie Pono as we left the Dream Kitchen. "Your Dream Maker is long winded! And very creative!"

## Data From Dakota17

Let's Hear it for the Imagination

Albert Einstein, who lived from 1879 to 1955, was a really smart guy. If you are interested in science and the philosophy of science, you will want to learn more about him. He was a fan of the imagination. Here are some quotes from him:

"I am enough of an artist to draw freely upon my imagination. Imagination is more important than knowledge. Knowledge is limited. Imagination encircles the world."

"Imagination is everything.
It is the preview of life's coming attractions."

"Logic will get you from A to Z;
imagination will get you everywhere."

Pablo Picasso, who lived from 1881 to 1973, was a Spanish painter, sculptor, poet and playwright. If you study Picasso, you will learn how often he changed his style and how much he influenced other artists. These words reflect his respect for the imagination:

"There are painters who transform the sun to a yellow spot, but there are others who, with the help of their art and their intelligence,
transform a yellow spot into sun."

"Everything you can imagine is real."

"We are what we pretend to be,
so we must be careful about what we pretend to be."

# 8. THE HEALTH AND HEALING CENTER

My Dream Maker escorted the group of us, Auntie Pono, Li'l D, Kid Dakota, me, and, of course, Imp, Thynk and Breeze out of The Imagination Factory. Mere moments after we left the Front Office of the Imagination Factory, a couple of heads peeked out the door of another office and called to us. "Hallooo!" they spoke in unison. "Good evening, Auntie. We are ready for your visit. We've got everything on automatic right now, so we can take a short break. Please, let's sit for a while."

The sign above their door read "Health and Healing Center Front Office". We followed the two doctors, a man and a woman, into a room with just enough light for us to feel comfortable and just big enough for all of us to sit in a circle. In the center was a glass bowl holding a glowing candle, set on a block of glass that reminded me of an ice cube.

No one spoke for a while, and that was fine. The longer we sat and watched the candle, the more sounds I was aware of. I especially noticed the whooshing of ocean waves and the beat of a distant drum. After a while, I noticed the random sounds of drips and dribbles and drizzles and realized that those sounds had been there all the time—I just hadn't noticed them.

Slowly it dawned on me that the sound of the ocean waves matched the rhythm of the air moving in and out my nose. I began to understand that the other sounds were coming from my own body. I could hear my blood moving and food digesting and my heart pumping. It was a percussion symphony - made out of me.

We all sat together just long enough for Li'l D to fall fast asleep. The doctors got up quietly. Together they opened the small door labeled "Health and Healing Center".

"We'd like to give you a little tour of our offices, and a better understanding of what is going on in your body," they said in unison. Breeze stayed with the sweet sleeping Li'l D while the rest of us glided through the door.

I was astounded to see we were in a huge medical laboratory. I did a double take when, in the center of the room, I saw a pulsating computer in the shape of a body...mine! It seemed to be breathing. The doctors showed us, on their huge flatscreen computer, that they could bring up information about one part of the body and then connect it to all the other parts of the body. They confidently assured us that they had programs that connect all the different functions of the body and other programs that release healing chemicals from inside.

"Let's not forget to mention our Healthy Life Center," one of the doctors said. "You've been doing a good job, Dakota, of collecting information about eating well and getting enough sleep and exercise, study and play. It may not surprise you to know that we often welcome Breeze to help out here. When you are feeling healthy and happy, you can send a nod of appreciation to Breeze for helping you to be in balance, and Breeze, in turn, will remind you when you are holding on to negative thoughts and beliefs."

Imp was now flying around the model of the body and waving to Auntie Pono. Auntie smiled and spoke directly to me and Kid Dakota. "Imp wants me to give you a cool idea that he says can be helpful. If you are sick or you hurt yourself, you might want to try it. You can do this any time of the day, but it's especially helpful right before you go to sleep. First, come up with an image of the very wise doctors in your Health and Healing Center and ask them to help with the problem.

"Explain the problem to them as clearly as you can and, with Imp's help, imagine what your body will look like as it's repairing itself and how you want it to look when it's healthy. For instance, say you stubbed your toe and it is still throbbing when you go to bed. First, pay close attention to the problem and send apologies, gratitude, and love to your toe, even though you're feeling uncomfortable. Ask your toe directly what it needs to feel better.

"Then, say something to your inside-self like, "Doctors, please remove whatever is in the way of healing my throbbing toe." Put all your attention on seeing with your mind's eye a picture of, for example, a bag of ice on your toe.

"Then, see yourself kicking a ball with that foot and feeling no pain. You might also ask your Dream Maker to send you a dream with information to help heal your body."

"Anything else, Imp?" Auntie Pono asked. Imp closed his eyes and tapped his chest. "Oh, right, of course. Remind yourself to use your cleaning tools until it becomes a habit."

When I heard that suggestion, I started repeating the words "Thank you, I love you" in my mind. I watched Auntie Pono, The Kid, and Thynk close their eyes and murmur the words. I closed my eyes, too, and for the first time, felt something I now think of as my Ho'oponopono vibration.

I felt relaxed and contented, grateful and loving. I believe that Ho'oponopono vibration is always with me. Sometimes it's easy to be aware of that vibration and other times it's not so easy, but I'm happy knowing that it is always available.

### Data from Dakota17

With Ho'oponopono, we not only take responsibility for the sacred quality of our mind, but also take responsibility for our bodies. Do you know that we have more cells in our bodies than there are stars in the sky? Every seven years, the cells in our bodies replace themselves. Millions of cells in our bodies died today, but our bodies created more than three hundred billion new ones. The body I had when I was Li'l D's age was not at all the body I had when I was eleven.

When you are sick or injured, it can be a good idea to get help from a doctor. You can be a big help to your doctor if you also work with your Inner Doctors. The idea of having an Inner Doctor is not a pretend fantasy. Most medicines try to copy healing properties we have naturally in our bodies or that we can harvest from plants. Before you go to sleep, ask your Inner Doctors to help you heal, and imagine your body healed and healthy.

Start listening to your body. It can send you messages from your subconscious. For instance, sometimes when people get a stomach ache, it is a clue that they are feeling scared. A headache may bring a message of anger or stress. Tight shoulders often are the result of having too many worries to carry. Of course, tears can be a message of sadness or happiness. Tears of grief release toxins from our bodies. The next time you notice pain or tightness in your body, imagine asking that part of your body, "What are you feeling and what do you need?" Then listen carefully.

# 9. THE OPERATING ENGINEER AND BEYOND

"Thank you, I love you."

The words kept going through my head. We may have stood there for three seconds or for three hours. When I opened my eyes, I saw that my traveling companions were also opening their eyes. We looked around at each other and suddenly broke out in laughter for no reason I can explain. I felt so close to Auntie Pono and, especially, to all these important parts of me I had just met, but who had known me my whole life.

We were led out of the huge laboratory and back into the Health and Healing Center Front Office, where Li'l D was just waking up. The gold ribbon that was Breeze began flying in circles around us. After a little while, we all started cracking up again because Li'l D was singing, "Love, love, love," in a very loud and sweet voice.

I don't remember ever feeling so peaceful, and I wouldn't have been able to stop smiling even if I tried. Even though my whole body felt calm, I was full of energy and was ready for more discoveries. I was getting used to Auntie Pono reading my mind and wasn't at all surprised when she said, "Okay, Dakotas, onward!"

Saying good-by to my Inner Doctors, I left the Health and Healing Center excited to realize I had new ways to help myself. Kid Dakota led the way to a silver curtain shimmering in the rosy light of Info Central. Above it was a lit sign saying, "Vista Point". Auntie Pono made sure we were all properly secured by tying one end of our rope onto a hook on the inside wall of the dome.

"No one knows exactly what the Realm of Awareness nor the Realm of All Possibilities looks like," she said, "but thank you, Imp, for creating pictures that make sense to a four-year-old mind and even more sense to an eleven-year-old mind." Imp magically created a flashlight and shone it on the silver curtain, then on the rope on the hook, and then on the "Vista Point" sign. "Right, Imp. It's because of you, Dakota's imagination, that we can make this trip at all. Let's venture even deeper."

She told us to walk slowly through the curtain so we could examine it a little. It was made of what looked like spider webs, only more delicate. The longer I looked at it, the more webs there were. One minute I saw the curtain as just a flat piece of material, and then I could see that it was layers and layers of webs, all connected to each other. I stared, captivated.

I'm still not exactly sure what I saw when I finally glided through to the other side, and when I think back to that time, I get different pictures. Thank goodness for Ho'oponopono. It's not a problem if my thoughts and memories change whatever form they are in. They are just passing through.

Auntie Pono directed our attention out, toward what she called "The Field". I saw the same Beyond I had seen from the redwood tree and through the windows in the dome. This Beyond was clearer than before. There were delicate webs that went out further than I could see everywhere I looked. Like the curtains we had just gone through, the longer I looked, the more layers The Field seemed to have.

Before us stood a huge smiling stick figure person with a bajillion arms and a huge head that reminded me of a little sun. She stood in a tube of the same rosy light I saw in Info Central, where I first met Kid Dakota.

Auntie Pono explained that this was my Operating Engineer and that we were seeing one way to understand how, through our energy, we are connected to everything. We watched as a rosy light from above seemed to be absorbed into her skin and then released back into the universe through her many hands. I could feel Imp scratching my head furiously. Gradually, I could see more of the view in front of me.

My Operating Engineer stood within arm's reach of rows and rows of computers and file drawers and bookshelves surrounding her. She was constantly lighting up connections between where I stood and intersections in the Field. Every one of her arms was in motion but she, herself, seemed peaceful.

"Your Operating Engineer," said Auntie Pono, "is constantly coordinating your body—your lungs breathing, your blood circulating, your food digesting, your balance keeping you upright, everything. She is always working with the chemicals in your body and stays in contact with your Inner Doctors. She's also the one who sends dream ingredients to your Dream Maker. That is just the beginning. Mainly, she secures the connections you have with everything.

I glanced at Thynk, who had the strangest look on his face. He said, "It's amazing to have all of this information in front of me, but it's also way too much to truly understand. I don't know what to think!"

Auntie Pono covered her mouth with her hand, but I could see by the twinkle in her eye she was having a good chuckle watching Thynk try to explain his conundrum. "Those books and files, those computers and all the lights on the web contain information about everything that has ever happened in your life," she said. "They also contain information you've had since before you were born. All your memories are stored there, even memories you no longer need and memories of things you may have tried to forget ever happened.

"Your Operating Engineer is in charge of every cell of your body and every cell contains the Realm of All Possibilities. This realm holds your memories throughout your body. Dakota, you have memories of this morning and you have memories of last year. And this may be hard to believe, but you also have memories of the day you were born, and the cells in your body have memories from before you were born.

"Your Operating Engineer", said Auntie Pono, "has volunteered to show you one memory. You may not be aware that it has troubled you for a long time. Li'l D, do we have your permission to see it?"

There was a part of me - probably the Li'l D part - that didn't want to see the memory. Kid Dakota glided over to us and said, "We can do this. It is just a memory. It isn't happening now. It's over. I can't tell you it won't be scary, but I can promise you that it isn't real."

Li'l D held Clowns Are Scary tighter than ever, but finally said, "Okay, but I'm just going to peek."

"Good idea, Li'l D," Auntie Pono reassured. "It is absolutely your choice."

With that, Auntie Pono nodded to the Operating Engineer. A huge screen silently rose out of one of the computers. Scene by scene, a vibrant video came alive before our eyes.

Everything on the screen was from the viewpoint of a very short person. The first scene was of my mother coming into my bedroom. She looked like herself, just a bit younger. Filling the screen, she hugged the little me, saying, "You're four years old today. We're going to the circus to celebrate."

Then the movie fast forwarded to the circus. Most of the people around us seemed very tall and everyone was smiling. I saw my little hand around a cone of cotton candy. It would come toward me, almost filling the screen. It was always smaller when it moved away from the screen. I can almost taste that sweet treat to this day. There was a monkey doing cartwheels on top of a white horse. I was entranced watching brave and skillful acrobats and trapeze artists on the screen. A band was playing music that seemed perfect for a circus. I could tell that, in this memory of my fourth birthday, I was dancing to the music, because the image on the screen kept going up and down and right and left.

Suddenly, everything changed. The screen didn't move at all. A yellow VW Bug had driven into the middle of the circus ring. The doors opened and clown after clown tumbled out of the tiny car. Their ugly white faces, their huge red noses, and their gross black eyes and lips made them look like monsters. They had horrible huge feet and walked like they were crazy. Their clothes were ridiculous-they were too big, and the colors didn't match. The clowns were acting wildly, spinning around, jumping in the air, squirting people with water from fake flowers and pouring confetti over them. From my perspective at four years old, those clowns looked way scarier than they did to me as an eleven year old. I could understood how scary it was for me when I was so little.

Breeze flew over to me and Li'l D, who had only gotten glimpses of the video but was, nevertheless, shaking like a leaf. Breeze touched our shoulders gently. When we both inhaled deeply, I realized I had been holding my breath. Breeze's touch reminded me that this wasn't real; it was just a memory - a memory from the eyes of a very young child.

All I could see were clowns laughing and cackling like crazy. I felt so much compassion for my younger self, who must have thought the clowns, with their weird menacing eyes, were staring directly at our family.

I understood right then, deep in my bones, that back when I was four, I was afraid that those clowns were about to come into the stands, grab me and take me away! On the screen, the image shook and a child's scream sounded louder than any of the other sounds of the circus.

"Mommy!!!"

The screen filled with the image of the palm side of my chubby little hands and glimpses of light between my fingers. My view of the circus and even of my family became blurry and the circus noises became quieter.

The screen showed the Li'l D me looking down to see my small hand clutching a scary-looking raggedy clown doll. When I was four, I had cleverly created, with the help of my imagination, a world that felt safer than the circus had. I could see on the screen that I had not only created Clowns Are Scary in my mind, but also a table to crawl and hide under.

Then the screen went black and quiet, showing me the moment when a part of me closed my eyes and ears completely to the outside world. That part of me was Li'l D, the part of my mind that stayed stuck in the fear and never grew beyond four years old.

I looked down and picked up my trembling four-year-old self. Auntie Pono whispered some words to Thynk and me, and I repeated them slowly.

"While I was growing up and learning all about the world, you have been so scared, stuck inside this memory. I am so sorry, Li'l D. Please forgive me. I had no idea you were hiding all this time."

Li'l D was trying to settle down. This was not easy!

"You were a very smart little child to create Clowns Are Scary," I told younger self. "You were learning that some things are safe and some things are not. From everything you knew until then, those clowns looked dangerous. You created Clowns Are Scary to remind you to stay away, so you could feel safe. You found a place under the table where you thought you would be protected. You're a smart little kid. Thank you for doing your best. We really love you."

As I was talking to Li'l D, I realized how very small and young I had been. I saw that I had made myself feel even safer by closing my eyes and covering my ears. I remember thinking, "I'm eleven, and here I am looking back and seeing how very little of the world I understood when I was four. Maybe my picture of the world right now is also very small compared to what it will be when I'm 22 and 44 and 88!"

Imp planted himself on my head and scratched behind one of my ears. When I looked up, I could see beyond the Operating Engineer, the computers, bookshelves and file drawers. Shimmering in the ever-present rainbow glow were millions of vibrating lights attached to infinite layers of delicate webs.

Auntie Pono explained that what we were seeing was just one way a human being can begin to make sense of the interconnected webs. "All these lights are connected. The closest are your closest relations, your family, your friends, and the landscape around you. Then come people in your community and all the people alive today. A little further out are the people who came before you and the people who will come after. All the animals and plants and minerals of the world, and then the universe, are lights in the Field. As are you."

I held hands with my four-year-old self and looked out as far as I could see. I was in awe to realize how much out there and in me there is. I have a whole world inside of me!

Auntie Pono's attention turned to Imp, who had just flown over to her and started waving his hands in front of her eyes. She held out her palm for him to land on. We watched as he made a big deal of breathing in and out. A cloud of sparkles entered his nose with every breath in and a lighter cloud was exhaled with every breath out. After a couple of breaths, Imp bowed deeply.

"Thank you again, Imp," she said, then leaned in close to Li'l D and me. "Dakotas, Imp wants me to show you something cool. Watch how your cleaning tool becomes a healing tool. Let the word "love" rest gently in your mind." As I did, I could see ripples or waves of pink flowing from me out to the Infinite Field. Parts of the Field started to open up like flowers opening to a spring rain.

"What you are seeing", said Auntie Pono, "is one way to imagine people, lonely scared, angry, or sad, unknowingly accepting the loving energy falling down upon them. "When you clean," said Auntie Pono, "you remove blocks and barriers so that your loving energy can go beyond just yourself and the people you know. It goes to where it is needed. There are people, animals and plants, alive and past, who need to feel that love."

Auntie Pono touched my shoulder and was quiet for a moment before she spoke again. "Even though you can direct your positive energy to a friend," she said, "when you take the responsibility to clean all the time, you can be sure you are helping the whole world. You will discover that the more your energy goes to healing, the more healing energy you will receive."

She continued to explain slowly enough that I could follow her. "The net you see is like an Infinite Field, as large as the universe. This is just one way we can understand that everything and everyone is connected, and each of us is a part of that Field that goes on forever. It is just one way we can understand the Divine.

"Speaking of Divinity," she said, turning around, "I believe it's time to make some decisions."

## 10. THE HEAVY BACKPACK

I took a last look at the huge Field, (that is, if "huge" can mean "infinite"). Auntie Pono said, "Right now you're seeing into the depths of the Realm of All Possibilities. Even with Imp's help, it's like looking at a line that is supposed to represent a cube. There is no way a human mind can understand it completely, but we can have a good time wondering. Wondering about the Mystery is part of the fun of life."

As she was saying those words, I had so much love for the Mysteries of Life. I could feel so chest filling up and expanding.

What happened next might seem weird to you. It did to me. But mainly, it was wonderful. Somehow, when my chest filled and expanded, my heart seemed to keep growing outside of my body. I felt an energy coming off me, as if the sun were inside me and radiating out of me.

Shortly, Auntie Pono called out to The Kid. "Lead us back to Info Central, please and thank you."

I could tell that Kid Dakota was getting a kick out of having such an important role. In a few short moments, still holding on to our almost invisible rope, we glided away from the mega-busy Operating Engineer, who didn't even look up. Auntie Pono opened the same curtains we'd gone through originally, and on the other side we got one more glimpse of the Health and Healing Center and the Imagination Factory. The door of the Imagination Factory was pulsating to the beat of the music inside.

As we glided along, I saw a colorful door I had not seen before. Its sign read "Child Care Village: All Kids Welcome!" I peeked in the window under the sign and saw kids playing in a park and older kids holding and talking to little ones. I also saw cradles, cribs, beds and cozy-looking chairs. There were toys and art materials. Kid Dakota moved close to Li'l D and said, "Later, I'll take you there. You just let me know when you're ready."

I can't speak for Li'l D, but I was excited about the idea!

When we reached the large space in Info Central where we had first met Kid Dakota, we let go of the rope. I had wondered about Kid Dakota's backpack and noticed that The Kid had never taken it off. It seemed to grow bulkier and heavier at different times during our expedition, and smaller and lighter at other times.

"Kid," the Thynking part of me said. "I feel so guilty that you have been carrying that backpack all by yourself this whole time." Even as I was saying this, I could see the pack growing. "Oh, now I feel guiltier!" I exclaimed, as I watched the backpack grow even larger.

Thankfully, Auntie Pono was there to explain and stop this out-of-control-thinking. She said, "Every time you have a negative thought or a feeling like guilt or shame, or when you think you know exactly what the future is going to bring, it's like you are putting rocks in The Kid's backpack. When you clean, the rocks become light energy, just as the deepest part of you - call it your Inner Divinity, your True Self, or your Higher Wisdom - is light energy. First, accept that The Kid's backpack is just the way it is supposed to be in this moment. Then, just clean."

I decided to try it.

Instantly, I found my Ho'oponopono vibration. I focused on that peaceful feeling in my body, that quiet hum. Feeling lighter, I watched The Kid's backpack became smaller and smaller. I decided immediately that I would be very careful to avoid letting thoughts stay stuck in my mind. They would only weigh down any of the younger parts of me inside, like rocks in a backpack.

Auntie Pono motioned Thynk to stand beside me. She gave a nod to Imp who had been happily treading air like a hummingbird. He jumped onto Auntie Pono's upturned hand and, with great aplomb, pulled a small scroll out of his hat. He displayed it in front of Thynk and me while Auntie Pono whispered over and over the words, "I'm sorry ... please forgive me ... thank you ... I love you".

She brought us all very close. With Breeze's ribbon encircling Thynk and L'il D, Kid Dakota and me, she repeated the mantra a few more I realized that my Ho'oponopono vibration was always there. It's a calm, quiet hum that helps me get in touch with peace inside me. The Kid's backpack got smaller and smaller until it was empty and flat.

Auntie Pono said, "Remember that image and out of respect and love for your inner little ones, avoid letting dark words and thoughts stay stuck in your mind. You are not only weighing yourself down, you are stuffing a whole bunch of rocks into the backpacks of your younger selves. Not Thynk's best idea!"

Instantly, I found my Ho'oponopono vibration. I focused on that peaceful feeling in my body, that quiet hum. Feeling lighter, I watched The Kid's backpack became smaller and smaller. I decided immediately that I would be very careful to avoid letting thoughts stay stuck in my mind. They would only weigh down any of the younger parts of me inside, like rocks in a backpack.

## Data from Dakota17

One thing we need to keep reminding ourselves is that our subconscious mind is always ready to take suggestions. We can choose to stay stuck in our memories or we can clear our minds and allow our subconscious and conscious minds to experience Inspiration.

When we choose to let go of the thoughts connected to memories, the lighter we feel. Then we are more able to receive Divine Inspiration, or in other words, our Inner Wisdom. The more we allow ourselves to be filled with this perfect, positive energy, the more we will be able to make positive choices and changes.

It was on the magical night that I first fell in love with The Mystery. I am learning to accept that I can't understand or explain it all, whether it be through religion or science. I guess you could say I am more humble.

## 11. CACA MOUNTAIN

I am astonished now to think that earlier I had not noticed a huge door beyond The Kid's desk. It looked like stained glass and it was immense. Just like every curtain and door I'd already seen or passed through, the top was impossible for me to see.

The light coming through the glass had the same beautiful warm rosy glow that had filled Info Central. I was sure it was the entrance to my Sacred Gardens. I was more than ready to go through that door, but Auntie Pono wanted to talk to Thynk first.

"Thynk, we are going to help set Clowns Are Scary free. Here is where your great intelligence comes in."

Thynk's eyes opened wide.

"Whenever a problem upsets Dakota, you have two options. One option is to face all Dakota's memories and feelings of the past. The other option is to let go of all of that."

"Whoa!" I interrupted. "It doesn't seem like such a good idea to erase all my memories. There are some happy ones, for one thing. Furthermore, without memories, school is going to be impossible. People have created a world of art and science with their knowledge and imagination. Why would we want to erase the memories of all that?" From the corner of my eye, I could see that Thynk was non-stop nodding.

I couldn't stop there. "What about uncomfortable thoughts and memories that teach valuable lessons? If they're forgotten, it could lead me to make more mistakes."

"You will not forget what you need to remember," said Auntie Pono, "or important events in your life. But too often you let uncomfortable thoughts stay stuck to your memories. It keeps your focus away from the present when you are sad or mad about the past or worried about the future. Check it out," she said, pointing to where we had just come from.

She pointed directly to a large door that wasn't apparent to me moments earlier. As she opened it, she said, "If you choose, you are free to hang out for as long as you want right over there at Caca Mountain. It can be quite an entertaining place to waste, I mean, spend time."

Directly from the door way, a path led to a mountain that looked like layers and layers of, excuse my language, cow patties. It stunk, though I have to say, the smell was somewhat familiar and a little enticing.

Auntie Pono explained to Thynk and me, "This is a typical Caca Mountain and it is all yours. It is created by thoughts and feelings that are still stuck to memories you have had or didn't have, yet are a part of who you are.

"If you want to get close and investigate," she continued, "you will find layers of anger, layers of worry and regret, layers of selfdoubt and layers of resentment. You will also find layers of fear, layers of anxiety, layers of arguments where you had to be right. I could go on and on.

"In or out?" she asked. "Your choice."

"The curious smell was rapidly becoming a stench. I had a terrifying image of Li'l D getting sucked knee deep into that mountain. "Please, close the door!", Thynk and I yelled together.

88

Auntie Pono slammed the door shut and the sight and stink of that mountain were gone. Feeling very wobbly, Thynk and I held on to each other. Gradually we regained our equilibrium.

"It's a no-brainer," said Thynk, turning toward our Sacred Gardens. "No question, I'm ready to let go of all of it."

Time stood still for just a moment. Breeze danced in the air above Thynk.

Auntie Pono whispered, "You have decided to focus your attention on Divinity, so I wouldn't be surprised if Divinity is already cleaning. Here's what I mean by that word.

"Divinity is a part of us and we are a part of it. It is us. It's female to some and male to others. For some, Divinity is both, and for others, it's an 'it.'

"To some people, Divinity looks like a clear blue sky. To others, it looks dark, like a huge night sky. It may look like a man with a beard or like a fairy godmother or an angel.

"For many people, what Divinity looks like changes as they get older. Many people don't see anything; they just feel something they may call 'love' or 'awe'. Choosing to face toward the Divine, to allow the Light of Divinity to fall on us, makes all the difference."

Auntie Pono's voice was warm and comforting. "The Divine has an agreement with us. It is always ready to heal our memories and uncomfortable feelings, but waits for us to give the signal."

I was just beginning to understand and I was still confused. I asked Auntie Pono what she meant by the signal? She replied, "Your Ho'oponopono cleaning tool is the signal. It is the key that opens the door that leads to Divinity. It is that simple. Are you ready?"

Thynk looked so confused. He scratched his head as Imp balanced on his hand like it was a surfboard. Breeze, twirling in the air, lightly touched Thynk's shoulders and then mine. At the same time, I felt all the muscles in the back of my neck relax. Weird.

"Know this, Thynk," said Auntie Pono, as she held his hands in hers. "At any moment you have the freedom of choice. One option is to run your life based on Dakota's memories and everything attached to those memories. The other option is to stand in the light of Love and to remove anything that might be blocking it."

Thynk made his decision. Imp grew little wings and fluttered off of his head. Thynk moved squarely in front of the large stained glass door, with his back to all the other doors, including the Imagination Factory, the Health and Healing Center, the Childcare Village and others we hadn't looked into. Thynk's eyes were closed and big puffy heart clouds were streaming off his head. Very quietly, Thynk chanted, "I'm sorry, please forgive me, thank you, I love you." Kid Dakota was holding Li'l D's hand and their eyes were closed. I wouldn't be surprised to hear that Auntie Pono, Thynk, Imp, Breeze and I were breathing together, in unison.

## Data from Dakota17

Auntie Pono used the words "Inner Divinity" for the Superconscious Mind. This is the part of us that oversees our conscious and subconscious minds. It is the part of us that has never forgotten that we are always connected to Divinity. The more we invite our Inner Divinity to be present in our consciousness, the easier it is to let things come and go without getting stuck. And the more we let go of judgments and expectations, the easier it is to enjoy the company of this Superconscious part of us.

The more we pay attention to the nonjudgmental attitude of our observing self, the closer we can consciously be to our Higher Wisdom. As we grow, we can begin to take more responsibility for holding on to the negative thoughts and feelings that come our way. We can be aware that they are there only because we have chosen to hold on to them in our conscious mind. We don't need to change the people or situations connected to our problems. It is the energy we have connected to them that needs to change.

We are all stardust! Carl Sagan taught many people about astronomy and other natural sciences. He explains, "The nitrogen in our DNA, the calcium in our teeth, the iron in our blood, the carbon in our apple pies were made in the interiors of collapsing stars. We are made of star stuff."

Another scientist, Neil deGrasse Tyson, agrees and says, "The atoms of our bodies are traceable to stars that manufactured them in their cores and exploded these enriched ingredients across our galaxy, billions of years ago. For this reason, we are biologically connected to every other living thing in the world. We are chemically connected to all molecules on Earth. And we are atomically connected to all atoms in the universe."

# Part Three

## Beyond the Beyond

### 12. BEYOND THE BEYOND

*A*UNTIE **Pono** broke the silence and said, "Look, everyone!" We all stared, wide eyed.

Breeze had used her ribbon form to slip through the keyhole in the huge door in front of us. The large shiny doorknob silently turned and the door began to open.

As the door opened wider, everything around us - Info Central, Kid Dakota's desk, the offices - faded away except for the door itself. Gorgeous gardens sprung up in their place. We walked through the door, just for the fun of it. We could have just as easily walked around it.

Kid Dakota set his dark glasses and earplugs down, saying, "Thank you, I love you." The rest of us set down our protective gear and thanked each piece for protecting us and making our trip comfortable. I swear I heard my glasses answer, "It's a pleasure, I'm sure." We unzipped and took off our suits of tiny mirrors.

In the blink of an eye all the gear disappeared, yet I wasn't surprised. I couldn't imagine feeling safer.

We seemed to be inside a dome that had walls made of limitless sky. The stained glass door was visible from wherever I went inside the Gardens. And from wherever I stood, I could see beautiful shining webs that went on forever.

I took Li'l D's hand and we ventured down an inviting path. Everything I saw took my breath away. There were all colors imaginable and others that I'm not sure I'd seen before.

We walked along more paths lined with herbs and flowers, passing small fruit orchards and bushes filled with berries. Everything smelled fresh and sweet. I knew many of these fruits and flowers, but had never known them to be so bright and vivid. We meandered past green lawns and small ponds, gentle waterfalls and fields of colorful flowers. Some were tiny, while others towered over us.

The awesomeness of nature filled my senses. We saw squirrels sitting in tree limbs and cracking nuts. We heard all kinds of songs as the birds flitted from fruit tree to berry bush. We picked and ate berries and our hands turned red from the juice. It felt amazing and from the look of Li'l D's eyes, I wasn't alone in that feeling. We wandered for quite a while, taking in the sights and scents and occasionally picking a berry or a cucumber to nibble on.

The path circled back to the center of the garden. Auntie Pono explained that these were my personal Sacred Gardens and that I could plant anything and go anywhere in my Gardens my imagination took me. We settled in an open area with benches on the edges, each one facing another entrancing view.

Auntie Pono took Thynk's arm and led him to several soft cushions under an oak tree. As he settled down, Auntie Pono thanked him for taking a break from his thinking job so that I could appreciate my Sacred Garden more. The rest of the time we were in the garden, he sat there cross-legged and very quiet, going in and out of, what seemed to be, a sweet peaceful sleep. If he was aware of what was happening, he seemed to have no interest in giving anyone a piece of his mind.

At that moment, I changed my attitude about Thynk. It was as if, when he sat down, I laid down my judgments about him. From out of nowhere the words came to me: *Thynk, I'm sorry I get mad at you and call you names like "stupid" and "slow poke". Please forgive me. Thank you for being so clever and helpful, and for making the Ho'oponopono choice. I love you.*

Auntie Pono invited me and Li'l D to sit on one of two stone garden benches. Don't ask how a stone bench can be so soft, but it was. Clowns Are Scary sat in Li'l D's lap while Imp hovered gracefully over us. Auntie Pono and The Kid sat on another bench nearby. Breeze twirled in place, then settled herself into a hammock between two trees.

Inside this special place, Auntie Pono's gentle whispers were just loud enough to be heard. "Here in your Sacred Gardens, Dakota, there is only Now. Here, you can be reminded of your perfection, no matter how many mistakes you've made, bruises you have on your body or what disabilities you have.

"I call your Gardens "sacred" because this is a place where you can feel absolutely safe. Only goodness can come in. This place is home base for your Divine Consciousness. It's sacred because when you are here, you can feel the love and healing of Divinity. Your Inner Divinity is always waiting for you, and you can come here anytime.

"Remember," she said, "there is nothing that separates the Divine outside from the Divine inside, only the thought that they are separate. Some thoughts are so big you can't erase them all at once."

"I'll think about that another time, okay?" I asked, feeling a little overwhelmed with the idea.

"Sounds good to me," Auntie Pono said turning back to Thynk, "For now, don't think, Thynk."

She looked at the very quiet Thynk and giggled.

# 13. BIG CHANGES

When we had all settled onto the comfy benches, Auntie Pono told Imp to give me an image of something or someone to represent my Inner Divinity. Imp made a flying leap from his bench and landed on one of my shoulders. He got to work scratching my head and created a floating screen in front of us.

I could feel Imp wrapping his arms around my head and resting his own head on top of mine. We started imagining what my Inner Divinity could look like. Instantaneously, we came up with many images that flashed on the screen. A picture of a fairy godmother appeared. It morphed into the image of an angel. Pictures I'd seen of Jesus, the Buddha, and my basketball coach appeared. Two great big hands filled the screen and then were replaced by the image of a magician, which, not surprisingly, looked a lot like Imp.

"For now," said Auntie Pono, "let's use your idea of two big hands coming from above." While she was saying those words, the screen dissolved. I closed my eyes for just a second and when I opened them, a ball of light was shimmering in front of me.

The light gradually took on the form of two huge hands. They were cupped next to each other and seemed very soft. My relaxed body gave me the message that there was nothing I could put in those hands that they couldn't hold.

At the same time, I could see another image directly in front of Li'l D. Li'l D's image looked just like Cinderella's fairy godmother, wearing a fancy purple cape and carrying a magic wand. She held her hands out to Li'l D as she twirled her wand over her head.

"Please, Kid Dakota," said Auntie Pono, "will you stand by Li'l D to share your confidence that it is okay to let go of Clowns Are Scary?"

The Kid looked proud and happy to have such an important part in helping Li' D let go of that scary memory. Kid Dakota jumped up and stood next to Li'l D.

Li'l D, with great seriousness, carried the old, dirty doll as if it were a precious jewel. It slid from Li'l D's hands into the hands of the fairy godmother who held it close, gently kissed it and placed it into the palms of The Great Big Hands. Immediately, I felt light filling my body—as if I had no body! It was as if I were made out of light!

While Clowns Are Scary lay in the palms of the Great Big Hands, big changes were happening. The many pockets in its costume started filling up with who-knows-what. The doll looked very different, or maybe that's because I was looking at it differently. For one thing, its eyes were twinkling, reflecting all the light and love around it. Now I could see that the doll looked more scared than scary.

Later, Auntie Pono explained what was happening when Clowns Are Scary's pockets started filling up. While I had been putting all my attention on watching Li'l D's old raggedy friend, my Inner Divinity was collecting, from nooks and crannies in my mind, all sorts of experiences and beliefs connected to useless memories of clowns. That's what was making that raggedy doll's pockets bulge.

Breeze left her hammock and danced gracefully above our heads. She reminded us of Ho'oponopono and good healing words for me to say.

"Clowns Are Scary," I said, "I'm sorry I've kept you locked up inside me all this time. I take full responsibility for that. Please forgive me. Thank you for being in my life and for trying your best to keep me safe from clowns. I understand clowns differently now, and I know other ways to feel safe. I love you...."

"...And we are going to set you free!" cheered Auntie Pono.

We were quiet for a few seconds until Kid Dakota began a slow, quiet chant directed to Clowns Are Scary.

"I love you, Clowns Are Scary. I'm sorry. Please forgive me. Thank you."

I joined The Kid and it didn't take long before we heard the sweet voice of Li'l D piping in. Thynk automatically started chanting in his sleep. Puffy heart clouds came off the top of his head and he had a hint of a smile on his face.

As we repeated the words, the Great Big Hands gently tossed the doll into the sky. I held Li'l D's hands and we both stared in awe.

The doll was like a trapped bird that had been set free. As we watched, it flew! Then, after a while, it stopped and just floated.

While I watched Clowns Are Scary calmly floating in the peaceful sky, I could feel parts of my body—parts that I wasn't even aware were tight—start to relax. My stomach unknotted and I could breath more easily. My shoulders let go of the tension I had held in them ever since a part of me hid away, hunched under a table. My arms were so light; they automatically reached up and I felt my whole body fill with joy.

At first, Clowns Are Scary was easy to see. That worn out yet still colorful clown doll stood out against the infinite sky behind. After a little while, its scared and scary expression transformed into a smile. Li'l D looked up at me and said, "Ooh, I feel all warm and soft inside. Look! Scary, Scary is happy!"

What had originally been uncomfortable thoughts and feelings turned into tiny sparkling lights that flew out of the clown's pockets and quickly disappeared. That ragged doll became smaller and fainter, so maybe it was floating away.

I love you, Clowns are Scary.

Finally, all I could see were the three big orange round buttons that had been on the doll's shirt. Before I knew it, they turned into pink heart buttons. That was all that was left of Clowns Are Scary...three small pink hearts.

Those hearts floated back toward the Sacred Gardens. They hovered for just a bit, then plopped right into the hands of our fairy godmother.

She magically attached a heart button onto the chest of each of us Dakotas. When the pink buttons touched Li'l D and The Kid, those two faded away, along with the buttons. I was enjoying being with them and must have looked concerned.

"Have no fear," Auntie Pono said. "Li'l D is in Info Central, hanging out with Kid Dakota. It is time for celebration!

"Parts of you were afraid of clowns for many years," she said. "When you cleaned the scary thoughts and feelings from your memory, those places became empty.

"Everything happens in the blink of an eye," she explained. When your Inner Divinity removes your old, stuck, useless, and toxic thoughts and feelings, those empty places are automatically filled with the energy of love.

"It's as easy as letting go of a feather. You will not forget that you were at the circus or that you were scared of clowns. Now though, fear won't be stuck to the memory anymore." As if I just realized I'd been holding my breath for a very long time, I let out a long, satisfying sigh, and let that fear go, once and for all.

## Data from Dakota17

Since that day, Kid Dakota has sent me many messages, sort of like mental videos or voice mail. Once I got a picture from The Kid showing me a mental image of a starry sky, which had more stars than I had ever seen in a night sky. Occasionally, out of the blue, usually when I'm drifting off to sleep, I imagine that awesome starry sky. Looking at that sky, I know I am looking out into forever.

Sometimes I see the hands, our fairy godmother, or the infinite sky that the Kid saw. Mostly I see only light, and although rarely, I've also had the experience that I am part of the light.

**Transmutation** is a word found both in science as well as Hawaiian spirituality. It can be defined as the action of changing into another form. In Dakota's case, fear was transmuted into love.

Auntie Pono told me that sometimes, like that day, I will be conscious of what I want to clean. She said it is fine if I choose to use other cleaning tools. I was relieved when she added, "Your understanding and your words for your Inner Divinity or God may change. Your imagination may give you other ideas of how and where to let go of negative feelings." Since then, all sorts of pictures come into my mind. Sometimes I see myself dropping stuff into a flowing river and sometimes I put them into a rocket ship to the sun. Thank you, Imp, my dear imagination!

Here is one of the things I learned from Auntie Pono about what happened to me that night: when I take responsibility to clean all the time, a magic happens very deep in my mind. When I put my worries, resentments, comparisons and judgments in the Hands of Divinity (or whatever I decide to call that healing part of me), my problems become more manageable. Auntie Pono reminded me that my job is not to know exactly what I am cleaning. My job is just to clean, and I can choose from many cleaning tools to help me do the job.

## 14. OTHER LIFETIMES

After Li'l D and Kid Dakota left my Sacred Gardens and Clowns Are Scary was transformed, Auntie Pono left me alone to enjoy the peaceful quiet. It was like my body was filled with a wonderfully calm, dark blueness. I could feel it in my brain, in all my cells, and in every tissue and organ of my body. At the very same time, I sensed the blue light surrounding me as if I were swimming in it.

I closed my eyes and with every breath I took, I went deeper and deeper inside the blueness. There was no past and there was no future. I was only in the present moment with that deep, dark blue light. In that short time, I saw so many incredible images, but that I can only put words to a few.

In this place, so deep inside myself, I knew I could remember every experience I'd ever had. There was, within me, a journey of knowing - a knowing that words could never describe. I was so much more than my body or my brain.

I remembered, without any discomfort, being at the circus when I was eleven. Time went backwards and I could remember when I was four. I remembered being born, looking up at big faces smiling down on me. I received so much love, just because I was me. I sensed myself going back in time.

Soon I floated in a pale pink light until, suddenly, I found myself looking at a scene in a country village. In the center of the village were women and children dancing on a small stage. Then came men and women demonstrating great tumbling and acrobatic skills.

Between acts, a clown walked among the audience members. He was tall and very skinny. His face was painted with the juice of berries and charcoal from cooled wood fires. Suddenly, I was aware that I had been that clown and that I had lived in France a few hundred years ago.

With that realization, I saw through the clown's eyes, as though we were the same person. I kept doing my job, which was to hold out a hat and ask for coins for the circus troupe. Occasionally, someone would throw a coin into the hat. Just as often, though, someone would throw a piece of fruit at my face. As the juice dripped down my face, all I felt was shame and sadness inside.

Suddenly, I moved out of the body of the clown-me and witnessed the scene from a distance. I saw myself as the clown. I laughed and did a silly dance, because that was my job. I also saw tears running down my face. Slowly the clown, the other people and the stage faded away.

I was beginning to know my eleven-year-old self in a new way. After seeing this image, I knew I couldn't be as judgmental as I had been when I was ten. I certainly couldn't hate clowns the way I once had.

I remembered not being in a body. I remembered being in a kind of a school where I learned of choices I had made during my many lives. I had spiritual teachers I loved and who loved me. I knew myself to be a spiritual being, though at eleven I couldn't have expressed that. In this sacred place, I knew I could never be harmed and that I was absolutely safe.

I heard a message from within me, from, well, call it my Inner Divinity, my True Self, Higher Wisdom or my Sacred Intelligence. "Dakota," it said, "I want to share a few words with you. I'm the spirit you were born with.

"When you call on me, you allow me to bring you healing and joy. Breeze is my messenger. She is your observing self. The more you sense her messages, the more you will know what it feels like to be centered, balanced, and connected.

"Look again at these Sacred Gardens you and I have created," I heard from inside. My eyes swept across the blankets of color, reaching as far as I could see. "Your Gardens look like this, in this moment. They are always within you and you can make any changes you want. You have a very active imagination, so now you may find the sacred wherever you choose. May peace be with you always."

Then I heard nothing, except for the twitter of birds, a babbling brook, and Auntie Pono, still sitting on the other bench, lightly snoring. At first, Thynk, Imp and Breeze were nowhere to be seen. Feeling a little lost, I called for them, waking up Auntie Pono.

"Don't kid yourself, Dakota," she reassured me. "They were with you before, they are with you now and will always be." With those words, Thynk, Imp and Breeze came back into view. The quiet mood suddenly changed when Thynk, still dozing, yelled in his sleep, "Hip, hip, hooray!"

Chuckling, Imp gave exaggerated high fives to me and Breeze. Abruptly, he stopped clowning around and turned to face me. Imp stared into my eyes and I stared into his. Time seemed to stand still. There really aren't words to describe it, but with Imp's help I will try.

It felt like a warm gentle wind was sweeping around me and over me and especially under me, blowing layers of dust and dirt off my body and old, stale thoughts from my mind. That's the best way I can describe how this wind was clearing stuff away from me. When the wind dislodged the stuff, it floated off and became part of the wind. The more the wind cleared and the more relaxed I got, the more I had the feeling that I was totally unique from everything, and at the same exact instance, I was totally part of everything.

For a moment, there was a "just me" and a "me that was a part of everything." There were two of me, and that was just fine. I looked at my reflection in the gold knob of the ever-present stained glass door of the Gardens and I loved the person I saw. Without all that muck, I wasn't living in the past and I wasn't fretting about the future. I was in the moment and I was my True Self, a very lovable, magical person indeed.

I often remember what I saw that evening when I took one last look at my Sacred Gardens. I thought of all the different ways Divinity can appear, and how we decided to represent it with the Hands of the Great Big Thing. Just a little bit away from where we stood, I could see Breeze twirling, dancing and leaping between each of those Great Big Hands. That memory alone can still bring me great peace and joy.

Auntie Pono gently shook Thynk awake. "Thank you, Thynk, for quieting down. When you stopped trying to convince Dakota that clowns are dangerous, Dakota was able to receive help from Inspiration, from Divinity, to let go of the fear. So, thank you."

"My pleasure," replied Thynk, as he stood up and stretched. Addressing the rest of us, he said, "Thanks, Auntie Pono. Thanks, Imp. Thanks, Breeze."

Auntie Pono laughed. Imp winked and smiled broadly. Breeze curtsied.

Auntie Pono took my hand, closed her eyes and reached toward the door knob. The Gardens faded and, in no time, she, Imp, Thynk and I were on the other side of the large stained glass door. I felt so clear headed and content. I was definitely not the same person I was before.

## 15. HOME

Imp lead Auntie Pono, Thynk and me as we retraced our path through my mind. We passed the shimmering silver curtain that led to Vista Point where I had met my very skillful Operating Engineer. I reached over to touch the curtain. It felt like cotton candy! I recognized the Health and Healing Center and the Imagination Factory when we passed, but there were doors and curtains I hadn't seen before. When I asked where they led led, Auntie Pono said she had no idea, but she was sure it was wondrous and that I could return another time.

We stopped for a while in the middle of Info Central. I was surprised to see four or five other kids there, sitting close to Kid Dakota. Probably no surprise to you, they all looked pretty much like me. Auntie Pono reminded me that I have lots of kids inside, each representing an important time in my life. I doubt the ever-serious and always-have-to-be-right Thynk would have understood such closeness before our Ho'oponopono adventure, but he was enjoying it then.

My heroic Li'l D was sitting on Kid Dakota's lap. They were tapping a little purple button in the middle of the big pink heart-shaped pillow. Auntie Pono explained that each time the button was pushed, it produced the energy of the mantra I chose to be one of my cleaning tools: "I'm sorry, please forgive me, thank you, I love you."

I doubt Li'l D knew exactly what was going on, but the comfort and attention felt good. When Li'l D got bored or distracted, other inside kids took turns tapping the button. Whenever the younger children stopped, The Kid was right there, tapping away. I got the impression that that finger could tap on that Ho'oponopono letting-go button all day and all night!

Li'l D saw us watching and slid off The Kid's lap to run over to me. I bent down to hug this younger me and whispered, "I'm so glad to know you now. You can call for me and talk anytime. Thank you for all of your help." In return, I received the biggest bear hug a four-year-old could give.

I felt so much love and appreciation for Kid Dakota. I had no idea how good it would feel to partner up with this part of me.

"So, Kid," I said, shaking hands. "You're going to remind me to take responsibility and admit when I make mistakes."

"Check," the Kid replied.

"And you're going to signal Thynk when he's out of balance with Breeze, like when he gets stressed and can't see the bigger picture."

"Check."

"And you're going to listen to Breeze even when I'm so stressed that I can't. Let's also keep figuring out ways you can signal me to remember to let go."

"Check and check."

"And when I'm asleep you're going to chant or sing or say, 'I'm sorry, please forgive me, thank you, I love you' or something like that."

"Well, not necessarily," said The Kid, stopping me in my tracks. "I'm thinking of creating a program that will keep you cleaning all the time. It may be particular words, but it may be a hum. Don't be surprised if you feel peaceful more often.

"Do me a favor," said Kid Dakota earnestly. "Take some time during the day or when you're going to sleep to notice what's going on within you. Get real quiet and listen for a hum or a tone. Keep giving me suggestions of sounds or feelings in your body that are in sync with Ho'oponopono and with love, forgiveness and taking responsibility. We'll work it out together over time."

"Check, check and check," I said, finally letting go of The Kid's hand. "Thank you, Kid. I love you."

"I feel your love. We're partners now," said The Kid with a confident smile and a fist bump. Light, puffy thought clouds from Thynk filled the air above us.

Auntie Pono interrupted the Kid and me. "This is an opportunity to remind you both, Dakota and Thynk, that whatever thoughts you have will go straight to The Kid, as well as other kid parts of you."

"What are you saying?" I asked.

"They're always close by. Keep it positive," she suggested. "Would you ever tell The Kid or Li'l D that they're not okay or not good enough?"

"No way!" I said indignantly.

"Then you best let go of those thoughts when you realize you're thinking them about yourself."

"Sheesh," I said, looking back at Kid Dakota. "I almost forgot to thank you, Kid, for finding Li'l D. I feel way stronger now that I know you're a part of me."

We hugged for a long time. Kid Dakota returned to the heart pillow with the built in letting-go computer, followed by Li'l D and Imp, who allowed himself to be rocked in the arms of the little four-year-old.

As Auntie Pono, Thynk, and I were leaving Info Central, I saw the sign for the Childcare Village and went in. I remembered when Auntie Pono explained that for every important event in my life, there was a younger part of my mind who lived that experience. I was impressed that a very imaginative part of me created this place.

It was such a sweet place. We walked along a path with cute cottages and pretty little gardens. There were picnic tables where kids were eating lunch or working on a jigsaw puzzle. There was a pond with a little girl rowing a boat. I could see, in a new way, what people mean when they say we have both feminine and masculine energies inside us.

Most of the children seemed to be in the playground that had every piece of fun equipment imaginable. Some of the kids ran up to introduce themselves. One told me he loves to play marbles with his buddy. Another told me she loves buttons and she could count them all day long. Two kids almost my age told me they love going to the swimming pool and pointed to an area just beyond the cottages.

Since that day, I imagine sending love to all those inside children, the brave and the timid, the male and female parts of me, even if they aren't absolutely clear in my conscious mind. I know they're there.

As we were leaving the Childcare Village, I saw a few kids hiding in the shadows and peeking out of windows. Auntie Pono whispered, "They are a part of you, too. Some are a little sad and some are a little shy. They're not sure if they can trust you. Give them time." I waved to them anyway.

In no time, we were at the bridge to the Conscious Mind, my Realm of Awareness. Auntie Pono and I stopped in the middle to take in the view. We looked down over the railing and saw the sparkling lights we had seen before. This time I understood it was the information - the data, the memories, the stuff, whatever you want to call it - that is always streaming into and out of the Realm of All Possibilities.

At the end of the bridge we saw the guards of the two realms again. Auntie Pono reminded Thynk that he and the guards at the gate are a team. "They are only doing what you and Dakota are instructing them to do and that's the good news," she said. "The more you make positive choices, the more your guards will be able to know when to allow information to come in or to block it."

Auntie Pono and I watched as Thynk approached the guard in charge of the gate between the Realm of All Possibilities and my Realm of Awareness. The guard stopped his work, just for the moment, and sat down cross-legged so he and Thynk were looking eye-to-eye. Thynk reminded him to have an open mind and to open the gate a little more every day. There were nothing but nods coming from that guard.

We waved to the other guard, the one protecting my little kid's inside from negativity and drama. This guard was working diligently to toss back the little balls of fluff, full of old memories and untrue thoughts.

With Imp's help I'm sure, Thynk pinned a gold ribbon on to the each of the guards' uniform. Every time I remember that scene, I think of my nonjudgmental Breeze. I take a deep breath, sigh, and immediately let go of a little tension.

Back in my Realm of Awareness, I no longer floated or glided, but was finally touching ground. I was only aware of Auntie Pono being with me. I was so exhausted that I leaned against her and let her guide me along a familiar path into my neighborhood, into my house and straight to my bedroom. I flopped onto my bed and Auntie Pono tucked me in.

"Thank you for walking me home," I said. Her reply was warm and comforting. "Dakota, actually, we are all walking each other home. So, thank you!"

As I began to fall asleep, I thought of Imp and Thynk and Breeze, grateful that they were part of me. I felt connected to my gate guards, L'l D and the many other younger parts of me. Auntie Pono hugged me and said, "You have been given the gifts of a conscious mind and a loving heart. Now you know that you are responsible for keeping them healthy and in good condition. This will be simple and effortless because you have also been given the gift of Ho'oponopono."

I didn't say a word, but I'm sure she knew that the great big hug I returned meant Thank you, I love you! And just before I fell asleep, I heard her whisper, "Good night, Dakota. Love, gratitude, forgiveness and freedom are yours forever."

## Data from Dakota17

Some things are beginning to make more sense now that I'm seventeen, but I still get confused a lot! For a few moments when I was eleven, I wasn't confused at all. I had experiences that were like pulling curtains open and looking out a window for the first time. In a short time, I consciously understood a part of Ho'oponopono that I deeply appreciate. Even though I may not always have those curtains open completely, I don't need any more proof that I am part of an interconnected web of everything that has ever existed.

I will never forget the moment that I saw fear turn into love. I still get afraid sometimes, along with all the other feelings people get. Sometimes I tell myself that I'm not good enough to try something new, and I make judgments or think other unhelpful thoughts. I remember, then forget, then remember again to clean. In those moments, though, when I was eleven and let go of my fear, there didn't seem to be anything separating me and the rest of the universe. There was a time in my Sacred Garden when I felt that when I inhaled, I was inhaling peace from the universe. When I exhaled, I exhaled love.

I thought about how the only moment that exists is this moment: NOW. The past is over and the future hasn't happened yet. Now is when life happens.

# Book Two

# Celebrating
# Ho'oponopono

# *Part One*

## The Pono Club

### 1. Awake

*I*'M seventeen now and I still remember how awesome I felt when I learned how simple it is to turn my fear into loving energy. Six years ago I went to sleep in a grumpy mood without understanding why. Now, since I remind myself of Ho'oponopono and my cleaning tools every night, I can't remember the last time I fell asleep in a bad mood.

The morning after my eleventh birthday, I woke up with a way better attitude than when I went to sleep. I didn't move a muscle for a long time, not even my eyelids, and just paid attention to my breath.

I felt full of the same lightness I had experienced in my Sacred Garden. Thanks to Imp, of course, I have an image of the dirty light bulb that Auntie Pono had described when we first entered the subconscious mind or, as she called it, the Realm of All Possibilities. It was as if I'd spent all night scrubbing years of gunk off my personal light bulb. I felt warmth and inspiration from that beautiful light.

I jumped out of bed and put paper, colored pencils and pastels on my desk. I got real quiet and invited help for ideas from Kid Dakota, Li'l D and, of course, Imp.

We drew sad clowns and happy clowns, silly clowns and really scary ones. I especially liked drawing scary ones. I knew I had discovered another way to clean, of letting go. With every drawing, I was letting go of useless feelings that had been stuck to old memories.

I never saw Auntie P.'s face again, but I heard her as I was falling asleep on the night I turned fourteen. She was laughing quietly. I started laughing. She laughed harder and then we were both laughing. I'm not going to clean off one bit of that one-minute memory. I'm going to keep it shiny.

Is there really an Auntie Pono? I like to think that the fascinating journey she took me on wasn't a dream. I asked myself, "How can she not be real?" Then again, I ask, "What is reality anyway?" Sometimes I wonder so much about so many things that my head feels like its spining. That's my clue that I'm feeling overwhelmed by all my thinking and that it's time to take a breath and let it all go. At least for a while!

## 2. THE PONO CLUB

A few days after my journey, I suddenly realized that the school's librarians, Stan and M'belle, had strongly influenced that nighttime peek Auntie Pono and I made into my mind. They had been visiting my homeroom class about once a month to teach us "cultural awareness" of people who live in the United States. They said that they wanted us to remember the ways we are alike and different and that there are many ways to have a good life. They wanted to teach us (I'm copying a handout here) to admit that we don't know everything, to suspend judgment, avoid making assumptions, and to have empathy (so we can imagine how people would like to be treated). It was especially important to them that we be comfortable with the complications and uncertainties of life (they called it "ambiguities"). They thought we must do more than tolerate the differences in people, we must respect and honor them.

They mainly talked about the beliefs of First Nation people (or Indians, as some still call themselves). We studied the original people from Alaska, California, the North American plains, the Southwest, the East and ta-ta-da!...Hawaii. I must have been storing more information than I realized, because, before I met Auntie Pono, we had a whole class on ancient Hawaii. That's when, about a month before my eleventh birthday, Stan and M'belle introduced me to Ho'oponopono!

We learned about an ancient legend that little children in Hawaii have been told for many generations. They say that when we were born, we came in to this world with a bowl of Perfect Light. We must take special care of this light by being kind, generous and forgiving. If we do this, we will grow to be strong and happy. If we become judgmental or jealous, it is as if we are dropping stones into our bowl of light.

Every time we drop a stone into the bowl, our Inner Light becomes dimmer. If we drop so many stones in the bowl that the light goes out completely, we will become just like a stone and stop growing. When we become stagnate, our Inner Light becomes dull.

When we are ready to fix the problem, all we have to do is take responsibility and be willing to correct our mistakes. We can imagine turning our bowl upside down and dropping all the stones out. When our empty bowl is upright, the light will shine again and can grow even brighter.

We modern people just imagine our bowls, but in ancient times grandparents carved a bowl for each grandchild. Children were expected to take responsibility for their behavior and put a stone in their bowl when they acted or thought in a way that would dim their true Inner Light. Later they would take their bowl to their grandparents to talk about what they thought or did. Then they would dump the stones out of the bowl so they could start again fresh.

Here's the part that I think is so cool about Ho'oponopono in ancient times: When the children took responsibility and apologized for their mistakes, their parents and grandparents also took responsibility for their part in creating the problem. Can you imagine if every time you made a mistake your teachers, relatives and friends would also take 100% responsibility and apologize for how they may have contributed to the problem? Maybe you can start the trend!

In one amazing night I went deep inside my mind and, at the same time, I could imagine seeing into infinity. After that night, you couldn't keep me out of the school library.

When I told her about my dream journey and about Auntie Pono, M'belle reminded me of Ho'oponopono and I realized I was in the right place. I started reading about it, and that's when I started learning how all the ancient aunties and uncles in Hawaii have taught their families Ho'oponopono for hundreds of years.

One thing led to another and soon I was learning about different religions and beliefs. I read on Wikipedia that, according to some estimates, there are roughly 4, 200 religions and sets of principles in the world. Sheesh! That's not counting personal philosophies about how to be in the world. (You'll see some of those teachings and philosophies in Book Two, Part Three of this book: Many Teachers.)

I got so excited learning about Ho'oponopono that I kept questioning Stan and M'belle about what I was learning. They suggested we invite other kids to come to the library to think, research and talk about Ho'oponopono. We decided on Tuesdays at lunch time. I put up some flyers and M'belle talked about it over the intercom during the morning announcements.

A few people told me they were interested, or maybe they were just wanting to be away from the cliques that form during lunch. We decided to call it the Pono Club, because we liked that the word means to do your best to treat ourselves, others, and the world fairly and with love.

Even though most of us are not native Hawaiian, Stan and M'belle encouraged us to adopt lessons from the ancient Hawaiians. They always reminded us that since we didn't learn these lessons from our relatives, we had a special responsibility to honor the ancient wisdom and have gratitude for the gift of Ho'oponopono. There are many English words for Ho'oponopono, but unless a person has grown up in the

Hawaiian culture, English words can't clarify its meaning completely. We talked about that and decided to accept that the best we can do is to be respectful and do our best.

Most people weren't interested in joining the club at all and some people made fun of us. They made fun of the word and called it hoo-hoo poo-poo. They said mean things to me and called me names like weirdo and loser.

Sometimes I would take it personally. Just one mean word would send me into a tailspin and I would feel down and depressed. One day, I told Stan how crummy I felt. I can still hear him saying, "That's great, Dakota, because it gives you just that many more opportunities to clean."

Some of my friends giggled when I talked about them being connected to everything, including their ancestors. (I didn't even tell them my ideas about already being connected to future people.) They guffawed when I said, "One hundred percent responsibility," and they snickered and pointed at me when I talked about Divine Conscious.

Believe me, I've had to clean tons of disappointment, anger, sadness and doubt about what other people think about me and the Pono Club. Really, though, who am I to say all those people should learn about something just because I think it's the coolest thing since cinnamon toast?

If I've learned anything, it's that there is a whoooollle lot more that I don't know than what I know. I know this though: Tuesdays in the library conference room at lunch time was often the happiest and most satisfying time of the week for me. There are four other kids, Jamie and Robin and Cori and Jadyn, who were in the club from the beginning. I wouldn't be telling this story without them.

Sometimes we were a quiet group and quite thoughtful. More often, we would all start talking at once because we were so excited about the ideas we were thinking about. The conversations we had, and the otherworldly adventures some of the other kids have had while they slept, could fill another book.

If you want ways to figure out how to be in the world, there are books and books of teachings and rules and stories. Many religions believe that their way is "The One Truth". That's why I like Ho'oponopono. It's easy. You don't have to give up your religion, but if Ho'oponopono makes sense to you, you can easily make the choice to live by its simple teachings. It's cut and dried: accept responsibility and keep letting go. It helps take the drama out of everything and life can become more peaceful.

# 3. SLO-MO-PONO

I told different parts of my adventure many times. Eventually, I could see the most important parts of my inner journey. With Ho'oponopono, the cleaning happens rapidly. The adventure we had was a slowed-down Ho'oponopono cleaning in which I could have compassion for a younger part of me, compassion for my problem, and receive compassion from my Inner Divinity and the Greater Divinity

Stan had an idea that we could take parts of what happened to me and have what he calls Do-It-Yourself Slow Motion Ho'oponopono Adventures. We all think it's a great way to let go of problem thoughts. We call Stan's creation Slo-Mo-Pono.

With Ho'oponopono, when we take 100% responsibility for our thoughts and feelings, when we use our cleaning tools, and when we let go of anything that isn't truly us, our problems transform in an instant. Although we can never know exactly what is changing when we clean, we can use this exercise to get an idea of how cleaning works—in slow motion.

It may look a little complicated, but it's really very easy. You will make friends with a younger part of you who will join you in making friends with a problem you share. The two of you will give the problem to your Inner Divinity who will give it to Divinity to fix. Use your imagination and give it a try!

# Instructions for Slo-mo-pono

Take a moment to sit comfortably and relax. Clear your head to allow your imagination to wander freely.

First, meet some important parts of yourself!

1. Imagine a symbol for <u>Divinity</u>. You may, for example, imagine the night sky, a man with a beard, a woman with a white flowing gown, endless light, or inspiration, itself. If you have trouble imagining your Divinity, you can borrow Dakota's (two big hands) or Li'l D's (a magical fairy godmother). Feel free to make up a name or choose another name, like 'God' or 'Love' or 'Universe'.

2. Imagine your <u>Inner Divinity</u>, the part of you that is never angry or worried or resentful. It is the perfect peace deep inside you. You may call it "My Higher Power", "Inner Wisdom", "Jesus", "Guardian Angel", "Fairy

Godmother" or "Inner Light". Your image of Divinity and your Inner Divinity may look exactly alike.

3. Imagine yourself as <u>a younger you</u> (any time from very young to yesterday) at a time when you were having some difficult feelings like fear or sadness or anger or shame.

4. Identify and name <u>the problem</u> you would like to release. This will be a thought, probably connected to an uncomfortable feeling or emotion. Examples of problem names are: "No One Likes Me," "I'll Never Understand Math" and "Clowns Are Scary and Dangerous".

Create a symbol of the problem which may be a negative feeling or thought. Ask your inner child for help with ideas. For example, Clowns Are Scary was symbolized by a weird-looking clown doll. Other ideas could be a jagged looking ball or a slimy creature.

# NOW YOU ARE READY TO LET GO!

**Find a comfortable place to quiet your mind, take a few deep breaths and free your imagination.**

1. **Ask your younger self, silently or out loud:**

   **"May I have permission to touch you?"**

   **If the answer is "yes", in your mind touch your younger self gently on the shoulder, on the hand, or wherever you think would be most reassuring to a younger you.**

   **If your younger self isn't in the mood to be touched, that's fine.**

   **Say, as gently and lovingly as you can, *something like this*:**
   **"Precious one (or your name), *I'm sorry* that you have had to hold The Problem (or the name you have given the problem) all this time.**

   ***Please forgive me* for not coming sooner.**

   ***Thank you* for being strong and helping me understand The Problem.**

   ***I love you.***"

2. **To the image that represents the problem, you and the younger you gently say *something like*:**

   **"Problem (or the name you give it), *we're sorry, please forgive us* for keeping you around so long, stuck in a place you don't belong.**

   ***Thank you* for trying to help us the best you could, because, in your way, you were trying to protect us.**

   ***We love you* and we are going to set you free."**

   **Take a few deep breaths and feel (or imagine you feel) the connection between you and Divinity (God, Love, Universe, etc.).**

3. **With your younger self, bring your problem to your Inner Divinity (or the word you have chosen).**

   **Your Inner Divinity will automatically include any memories connected to The Problem (or your word) that are ready to be cleared. For example, Dakota's fear of clowns may have extended to all strangers. Tossing out the fear of clowns helped Dakota**

be more confident with strangers in general. Chances are you will not be aware of what all the specific memories and stories are that you have created about those memories are, and that's a good thing.

4. Create an imagine of your Inner Divinity giving the problem to Divinity. In your mind, imagine your image of The Problem against the background of Divinity (or the word and image you choose) and notice how it changes. This may not take much time, but don't push yourself.

Many things could happen now. If the image doesn't change, let it get smaller. Watch it as it moves away from you and disappears or transmutes (changes, transforms) into a more positive image.

When you took away the problem, there were places that were left empty inside of you. You may see nothing. Just allow yourself to feel the peace inside.

Watch to see a symbol of positive energy returning to you. Imagine this positive energy filling the empty places where you had been holding all the negativity energy released.

## 4. THE HO'OPONOPONO CELEBRATION

At the end of the third year of the Pono Club—the year before I moved on to high school—Stan and M'belle suggested we have a party to celebrate Ho'oponopono. Instead of meeting on Tuesday at lunch like we usually did, we met after school. When the word got out that we were having refreshments and anyone could come, a bunch of kids we knew showed up at the library. I was surprised that they were so friendly to me, after assuming that they didn't like me for so long (ah, my problem!). Ho'oponopono! I don't know everything!

First thing, Stan taught everyone to say Ho'oponopono. "Say 'pono'," he said. "Say 'ponopono', say 'o-ponopono', say 'o-ponopono'. Say a real fast, short 'ho', almost like a hiccup. Say it again, 'ho'. Okay, 'Ho'oponopono', 'Ho'oponopono'!"

M'belle handed out the instructions for slo-mo-pono and, with my permission, of course, explained it, using the examples from my own story: Li'l D, Clowns Are Scary and the Two Big Hands.

I explained that at every Pono Club meeting we always took about ten minutes to write in our journals. We'd write about problems and how we might use Ho'oponopono in our lives, and about what we needed to let go and what we were having trouble letting go of. That ten minutes was all the journal writing some kids did. Some of us took the journals home and wrote everyday.

At the Celebration, most of "the Originals," as Jamie, Robin, Jadyn, Cori and I like to call ourselves, agreed to share some of the things we'd written. We had worked on our talks for a couple of weeks before the Celebration and, thankfully, Stan recorded the speeches, so I can share them verbatim, word for word. M'belle put each of our names on a card and picked them at random to decide the order of our talks.

Cori was first. "I've been thinking about how being born in this human body is pretty much a miracle. I could have been a lizard or a penguin. I could have been my weird cousin, Pat. Or I could never have been born at all.

"I am so grateful to have a body that can enjoy juicy oranges and swimming and listening to loud music. When I think of Ho'oponopono, I think about keeping my mind in good shape, but I also think about my responsibility to take care of my body.

"Lately I've been thinking about things that are not so comfortable, but are really important. Like when the flame from a candle burns your finger, it hurts. Sometimes I try to feel grateful for that pain, because it helps me to move my finger from the danger. Being hungry may not be comfortable, but otherwise we may forget to put food in our stomach.

"Stan reminds us that we may not have come into this life with everything working. We may be blind or deaf or our muscles may not work very well. When we are born we are perfect little beings, light beings. We are an expression of the Divine and our true selves can be nothing less than perfect. Stan told us to look at little babies and notice how they don't think about the past or imagine what the future will look like. They go from one emotion to another without judging themselves or other people.

"I'm a miracle, the one and only me, and I am pretty awesome!" Cori took a breath, and the whole room broke out in applause.

Cori took another breath and continued, "The other day, I figured out a cool way to handle my nervousness before a math test, thanks to my personal Imp. First I imagine my jitters as a very dark wiggly spiked ball, like a bowling ball, but with sharp spikes. Then I imagine I have a kind of paintball gun and after one or two paint splats, the heavy ball turns into a yellow tennis ball which starts bouncing around.

"It's weird, I know, but now I'm more excited than scared to take tests, because I usually do a good job of studying and I know the material. Now I feel a lot calmer and even have a little fun taking math tests. Ho'oponopono!

"I told my dad about Ho'oponopono and now he says 'Ho'oponopono' all the time. When he plops down on a chair, instead of letting out a sigh, he says 'Ho'oponopono'. Sometimes he walks around the house and sings it. I'm glad he does because I can use the word 'Ho'oponopono' as another cleaning tool. He's pretty funny. One day he pretended to get very serious and told me that Ho'oponopono is an ancient Hawaiian word for 'Oh, well!'

"I had fun doing slo-mo-pono. My Divinity looks like blue sky with fluffy white clouds and my Inner Divinity looks like my grandpa.

"The yucky stuff I want to clean are the terrible pictures stuck in my mind from seeing a train accident when I was little. The train was going too fast around a bend and some of the cars tipped over. No one was killed but some people got pretty hurt. My thought is that I will never stop thinking about what happened. The thought is connected to fear.

"I see myself as I might have looked that day. The little Cori, my younger scared self, is wearing footie pajamas and holding a toy train with its wheels dangling.

"I say to the younger me, 'I'm sorry that you've been so scared all this time. I hope you will forgive me, little Cori, that I have kept this fear inside us crammed into that toy train all this time.I can see you were so scared when you saw that train wreck. Thank you for being here to help me let go of the fear. I love you.'

"To the toy train I say, 'Fear, I'm so sorry that you have had to stay in this messed-up condition inside me all this time. Please forgive me. I know you were trying to help me by warning me of danger and I can tell you now, the danger is over. I love you, and I'm going to set you free.'

"When I imagine my grandpa in my slo-mo-pono, he picks me and the Little Cori up in his arms. When Little Cori hands him the wrecked train, grandpa sets us down and holds the train in both hands. He fixes the wheels and puts the train on a cloud shaped like train tracks. The train goes silently down the track and into a tunnel made of clouds. After a short while, a cloud shaped like a train comes out the tunnel right into my grandpa's hands.

"He sits in a rocking chair holding the train and closes his eyes. After that, I get an image of a little me on my grandpa's lap, sleeping soundly, holding a pillow shaped like a train engine with a big cartoon smiling face.

"When I did this slo-mo-pono, I noticed my arms and shoulders suddenly felt more relaxed, like I'd just put down a heavy load."

Cori was glad to be the first and to be done with the speech. As the group applauded, M'belle picked the next card and the next speaker. Robin jumped up and started sharing.

"I love, love, love my science class," Robin said. "I'm learning how awesome we humans are. Now I want to do lots more research. I learned that before we were born we began experiencing the physical sensations that come with being in a body. Wow! If you think about it, before we were born we were in a body (ours) inside a body (our mom's).

"Just think, when I was in my mother's womb I had the sense of smell and taste. I could hear sounds. This may sound gross, but I read that we can smell everything our mothers ate or inhaled and we could taste the amniotic fluid that we were swimming in. Being human is awesome. For me, learning about it is like being in the middle of a mystery story and I want to know more.

"Here's a story my mom told me that she says shows how loving and forgiving I was when I was three years old. I had a tricycle that I loved to ride. I rode on it all the time. My mom told me that I was a very fast tricycle rider for a three-year-old. One day I was racing around my backyard and drove over a crack in the cement walkway. Before I knew what was happening, the trike flipped on its side, and I fell onto the hard walkway. My first reaction was to say, 'Ouch!' Then my mom said that I got up, rubbed my skinned knee and went straight to the trike. As I was setting it upright, I told it, 'Oh, I am so sorry. I hope you are okay.'

"My mom says I hugged my tricycle and whispered, 'I love you.' Wasn't I cute? I was living Ho'oponopono when I was three!

"When I'm saying, 'I am sorry, please forgive me, thank you, I love you', I wondered, at first, who am I saying it to?

"This is what I understand so far. First off, I don't have to be thinking of anyone or anything. Stan and M'belle have explained to me that one of the ways Ho'oponopono makes life easier is that I don't have to be in charge of exactly what is being cleaned or who I'm directing my words to. I can even imagine I'm hearing them from my Divinity.

"I've done a bunch of slo-mo-ponos, and here's how my first one came out. Divinity sometimes looks to me like a big oak tree with lots of branches. My Inner Divinity looks like an angel.

"I had just moved into town when I started sixth grade. This school, the kids, everything was so new for me. I missed my old friends and it's hard for me to make new friends, so sometimes I would jump to conclusions and decide that people didn't like me. I'm glad I found the Pono Club, because I was feeling miserable. The yucky stuff I wanted to let go of was of feeling lonely, little, and powerless.

"I imagined myself at the beginning of the school year with a bag over my head. I could see out, but no one could see me. When I imagined my angel, the bag lifted off my head and floated out to the tree. It got snagged on one of the branches.

"The bag floated back to my angel who reached and—I know this may sound strange and a little gross—pulled muscles out of the bag. The angel plopped those muscles on my arms and I felt stronger and more confident.

"That slow-mo-pono made a difference at school. The more confident I feel about myself the easier it is to be friendly with other kids."

The next person up was Jamie, who high-fived Robin as they passed each other. When the applause ended, Jamie began.

"The more I think about the opportunities I have because I am a human being, the more gratitude I feel and the more responsibility I feel to use Ho'oponopono." Jamie beamed. "Here are some of my thoughts about being born in a human body.

"I wear glasses because I can't see as well as other kids, but I'm pretty sure my sense of hearing is stronger than many people. I like to think of all the things I've been able to hear... all kinds of music, a friend laughing at a joke, rain on the roof.

"Sometimes I'll close my eyes and walk around my house just using my hearing. There are always sound clues - my stepdad puttering in the kitchen, my mom's radio in her office, the sounds on the street. It is not that easy sometimes and I end up being grateful for the sight I do have, as well as my super hearing.

"I also have a great sense of smell. I'm grateful for that because I can smell my mom's delicious lasagna or when the milk's gone bad.

"Last night I was thinking about how Ho'oponopono tells us to take 100% responsibility for our actions and I remembered a feeling I had back in the fifth grade. I'd finally gotten permission to ride my bicycle to the park by myself. Before I left the house, my mom reminded me that I would have to be a responsible cyclist, but she hadn't needed to remind me.

"I'd been thinking about riding alone for weeks. I had to wear a helmet, of course, and check to make sure my shoes were tied. I finally passed her test to see if I remembered all the bicycle rules and laws, like using hand signals and what to do at a stop sign. I also knew to be aware of other bikes and pedestrians and cars, especially the ones that were not paying attention or following the rules of the road. When I was littler, it seemed like lots pressure to remember everything, but by that time, it was more comfortable.

"As I rode to the park, I was paying attention to my surroundings and, at the same time, feeling how wonderful it was to be riding my bike. The words that kept going through my head were, *I'm free! I'm free! I'm free!* I think this is an example of taking one hundred percent responsibility. The freedom I felt was like a gift. Now I look for other ways to take responsibility when it isn't even expected of me.

"Here's my slo-mo-pono: my divinity looks like the night sky with lots of stars and my picture of the Inner Divinity looks kind of like what Jesus might look like. It isn't exactly the Bible Jesus, but he is a very kind and wise person.

"Here's my yucky stuff to let go of: even though they say it's not true, sometimes I still think it's my fault that my mom and dad split up. I was always getting in trouble when I was three, so, not having much understanding of what the whole divorce thing is about, the guilt is still being clutched by that three-year-old inside me.

"I imagine myself sitting alone in my room, looking down. On my lap is a teddy bear with a sign around his neck that says 'Bad Bear'.

"When I give the bear to the Jesus guy, he immediately takes the sign off and replaces it with another sign that says 'Awesome Bear'. He tosses the bear up in the air and I can see it against the night sky. After a little while I see a beautiful light in the shape of a bear. My sadness and guilt are replaced with this bear's love. I feel like I was smiling inside.

"The bear grows little wings and flies back to the Jesus guy who cuddles it. After a while I see many little teddy bears doing summersaults on a big cloud.

"I sometimes feel that guilt, but now the guilt reminds me of all those playful bears. The playful bears remind me of how young I was. I believe my parents when they say it wasn't my fault. There's a difference between being responsible and feeling guilt. It's up to me to make sure that Awesome Bear stays with the little three-year-old me."

Even though every speaker had been applauded, Robin seemed genuinely surprised, pleased and a little overwhelmed to be the recipient of all the enthusiastic clapping. M'belle picked up a card and invited Jadyn to take the stage.

Jadyn began right away. "I usually feel very irritated when my baby brother gets into my room and messes up my stuff. I want to pound him!"

Jadyn waited for the laughter to die down. I guess kids could relate to Jadyn's problem. "Last night I decided to try Ho'oponopono my way. First, I took responsibility for the problem, and admitted to myself—and now, to all of you—that I hadn't completely closed my bedroom door and he was just being a little kid.

"After I closed the door, I completely filled my mind with the words *Thank you, I love you* over and over, as I rearranged my books, legos and some other toys. After a just a few minutes, I felt calmer and not so angry at my brother. In fact, I felt forgiveness and love toward him. And the room was actually neater than it had been before he invaded! Ho'oponopono!

"I have different pictures in my mind of what Divinity looks like. My picture this time is a big soft woman with skin the color of chocolate milk. I have the same picture for my Inner Divinity. My best friend's name is Ashanti and her grandmother is Mikalii. My image of my Inner Divinity looks just like Mikalii, because I think she is probably one of the kindest people in the world.

"The name I gave the problem I want to let go of is 'I'm Not Good Enough'. It appeared when my baby brother was born and it seemed that he took most of my parents' love and attention. Now, sometimes I think he exists only to bug me. This thought is connected to anger and sadness.

Jadyn was quiet for what seemed like a long time and then began to speak slowly, "My image is of my mom and dad giving all their attention to the new baby and ignoring me. I'm holding a doll with a sad face that looks like me. It's dirty, like it's been dragged in a mud puddle. I'm holding the doll by one foot and I'm not paying attention to it, just like no one is paying attention to me.

"I imagine Mikalii in the sky with a big, old wash basin and she tells me that we have a contract. She says her job is to clean anything I give her and she will, but I have to fulfill my part too. She says, 'You have to give me your problems. I cannot do it without you.' She says that it's fine with her if I give her lots to clean, because the more I let go of my stuff, the better she can do her job.

"I hand her the doll and she dips a wash cloth into the basin and very gently wipes the dirt off. When she is finished, the doll actually sparkles. After a little while, the doll disappears and all that is left is a heart of sparkles. She holds the sparkling heart over my head and sparkles fall all over me.

"When that happened I could hardly remember being angry at my brother. Now, I have images of him clowning around and making everyone around him laugh. I'm glad he was born."

As the applause died down, Jadyn picked up the last card and introduced me. "Heeeerrrre's Dakota, the very first member of the Pono Club!"

I couldn't believe it! The room exploded with applause. I was glad I had rehearsed my presentation with Stan, cutting out and adding parts, and practicing speaking in front of people. When everyone settled down, I started my speech.

"Love is cool. I can love my relatives and my friends, all in a different way, but I can also love a sunny day and I can love music. Sometimes I send love and gratitude to all my memories, especially the crummier ones. I like that I don't have to know exactly which memories to clean. I know there are always memories, even memories of ancestors, to clean. I say to myself and to them, 'And now I will set you free!'

"Remember Kid Dakota? The Kid is a really caring part of me inside that's always ready and willing to help me. I have pictures in my mental scrap book of my journey and one is of Kid Dakota carrying the backpack for me and some of the little kids inside who have had a difficult time in the past. The backpack could be full of fear, sadness and resentment. It could also be empty. It is my responsibility, to keep that backpack as light as I can.

"I know that when I clean, my positive energy is reaching beyond my conscious mind; in other words, that part of me that is awake and aware and able to understand what is happening around me. Because it is beyond my consciousness, I will never know exactly where my positive energy is going or what or who is receiving it.

"You heard my story so I'll just share my favorite cleaning tool. It's saying or thinking the words, "I'm sorry, please forgive me, thank you, I love you."

'I'm sorry' reminds me to take responsibility and not to blame other people - ever. Before, I thought everything was *outside* of me. Now I understand that it's all *inside* me. It doesn't mean that I am to blame, just that I am the only one who is responsible for my feelings and thoughts about what happens. Now I understand that if I think there's a problem, the problem is inside me, and it is something in me that needs to be cleaned.

"Sometimes I catch myself blaming people and sometimes I probably don't even notice I'm doing it. Like they say, there's no point in being mad at myself or impatient with how slowly I learn, because I would just have to clean those thoughts and feelings. So, why add to my list?

"'Please forgive me' reminds me that I'm always in a relationship with someone or something. It could be a friend, Divinity, a part of my body or the chair I'm sitting in. I'm asking forgiveness for whatever it is in me that may be responsible for the problem. I notice that the more I say the words 'I am sorry' or 'Please forgive me' to myself, the easier they are to say to other people.

"Before I heard about Ho'oponopono, I was confused. Now I see that I can take responsibility for something and at the same time forgive myself or another person. It feels sooo much better than holding on to guilt or anger or blame.

"'Thank you' reminds me of how much I have to be grateful for. I like writing in a gratitude journal. I feel even more grateful when I see my words of gratitude on the page.

"'I love you' is the reset button that reminds me of how even the scariest, saddest memories and feelings can be healed with love."

My speech was done. It felt good.

After my sharing, M'Belle handed the club members copies of The Ho'oponopono Choice. Even though we know that it's totally a personal commitment, we made a big deal of signing our copies with our fanciest cursive.

# The Ho'oponopono Choice

I choose to remember that my purpose on Earth
Is to know, to be, and to express my True Self,
By valuing what is important to me and honoring
The same worth in all beings.

My thoughts and feelings are not who I truly am.
I understand that I will always experience
thoughts and feelings, and
I recognize that my responses to what
happens in my life are totally up to me.
I choose to take 100% responsibility
for all that I am aware of and
I am willing to mend my errors.

I am grateful for the opportunity
To experience life in a human body,
With a loving heart and a creative mind.
I choose to express my gratitude
By remembering to clean all the time,
Letting go of information, thoughts, and feelings
That are not my True Self.

Before we ate, M'belle said, "We want you to know about a very important person. Her name is Morrnah Nalamaku Simeona and we have her to thank for creating a way for you and me to clean and use Ho'oponopono to help ourselves, by ourselves.

"This is Morrnah's Prayer that she gave to the world to use," said Stan, as he and M'belle reached their arms toward the sky. He began,

> "Divine creator, father, mother, as one...
> If I, my family, relatives and ancestors
> Have offended you, your family,
> Relatives and ancestors
> In thoughts, words, deeds and actions
> From the beginning of our creation to the present,
> We ask your forgiveness...
> Let this cleanse, purify, release and cut
> All the negative memories, blocks,
> Energies and vibrations,
> And transmute these unwanted
> Energies into pure light
> ...And it is done."

After Morrnah's Prayer, M'belle continued with her own blessing for us. She began with a fun way to say 'Divinity',

> "Dear Great Big Thing, we are about to have some celebration snacks. Please help us clean anything that might not be pono, good, right or healthy, so that we and our food may have the best energy possible. We pray for a Ho'oponopono cleaning, for healing and forgiveness, love and gratitude,

for everyone and everything involved in getting these treats to us.

"We pray that we may fully appreciate and honor the farmers and workers from all over the world who grew and harvested this food.

"We ask for healing for the truck drivers who carried the food and the people who made their vehicles. We ask for healing for the grocery stores, the farmers' markets, all the clerks and baggers who were part of getting the food to us and the families and ancestors of all these people.

"We ask that this blessing be given to all the parts of our bodies involved with this food and to the table and the chairs, the bowls and napkins. We thank our bodies for using the nutrients in the food to keep us healthy, give us energy and help us to let go of what is not us. We give thanks to the water and all people who help to bring us clean water."

She was quiet for a moment. Then she said, "Dig in!"

We chowed down on hot chocolate, cookies and apples, vegan, gluten-free crackers, orange juice and popcorn. And, my favorite, M&Ms.

Jadyn broke the silence with some cleaning words, "Thank you, popcorn" and a little later, "Sorry about this, apple. I love you!" Chomp.

We relaxed and told goofy jokes, like this one that M'belle made up: Why did everyone fall asleep when Stan told us a joke about The Infinite Field? It was endless.

When it was time to leave, M'belle gave each of us, even the new kids, a gift as a reminder that we all have an observing self or witness. "The observing self is a part of our mind that can see the big picture and is aware of whatever we are thinking, feeling or doing," she reminded us. "The more we pay attention to it, the more we can observe what is going on rather than react automatically to it.

"Dakota's observing self named herself 'Breeze'," M'Belle said. "Sometimes she made herself appear to Dakota as a dancing girl and sometimes she appeared as a golden ribbon."

She then gave each one of us kids a ribbon, gold and silky and as long as our arm. "When you see or touch or even just remember this cleaning tool, let it remind you that there is nothing that separates you from Divinity and that it is time to let go of what is not truly you."

Stan had a gift, as well. He handed each of us a folded card he had made.

On the outside was this:

**The answer to all your questions about**
# HO'OPONOPONO

On the inside were these words:
# JUST CLEAN!

# *Part Two*

# Easy Meditations and Visualizations

**D**AKOTA17 here. Stan and M'Belle introduced the Pono Club to meditation almost from the start. This chapter includes very simple meditations and visualizations we learned when we were in middle school and some that I've learned since.

Meditation is being right here, right now. It is being present in the present moment. With meditation, you can learn to merge your conscious mind (the state of mind you are currently in) with the power of your deep subconscious, sometimes called the universal mind.

I meditate pretty regularly now, but before the night that changed everything, I thought meditation was weird and boring. I never understood how it could be so simple and relaxing. The more I accept myself, the more I relax, and that helps my meditation.

Every time I meditate it's different. Sometimes I can focus pretty well. Sometimes Thynk is chattering nonstop. I know it is my responsibility to help my thinking become more quiet. I have noticed that when I start to pay attention to different

147

parts of my body, when I am sending love and encouragement to younger parts of myself, or when I'm paying close attention to the sounds I hear, Thynk becomes quieter and more content.

With the help of your subconscious mind, Ho'oponopono can be an all day meditation that is done in any moment, wherever you are. Your Ho'oponopono practice will improve when you meditate in other ways as well. My advice is to always treat yourself gently when you meditate. You may strive to improve your meditation but never, ever judge your meditation skills.

There are many ways to meditate. It is said that the Buddha declared that there are 10,000 doors to meditation. Some people meditate by listening to or making music. Others draw. Others walk in nature and focus on noticing everything that their senses are experiencing. You have your whole life to explore meditations.

# Meditations

## 1. Meditating, Letting Go and Becoming Aware

When you meditate, you might invite any of your own inner children who want to join in to meditate with you. You might consider these to be the parts of you that are feeling shy or scared or overwhelmed. The calmer you are, the calmer they will be. You may want to set a clock so you aren't distracted by time. Twenty minutes may seem like a short or long time, but it is always the same by the clock.

At first your meditations may be short, even just a minute long. You can add a few more minutes each time you sit, until you are meditating for 20 minutes or more. Don't push yourself too hard, but don't baby yourself either.

Find a quiet place to sit where you will not be disturbed. It's fine to sit cross-legged on a pillow or to sit in a chair. You can even stand still or walk very slowly. You can also lie down, but it's possible that you may fall asleep.

Sit as straight as you are able and, if you are sitting on a chair, place both feet firmly on the ground. Simply focus, without judgment, on keeping your back erect and shoulders relaxed. If you are someone who is not able, focus on an image of yourself sitting straight.

"Your posture is important. Since you may be beginning, or continuing, a life-long meditation practice, you would be wise to commit to this meditation for at least a month.

Gently close your eyes. If it feels more relaxing to you, you can half close them and let what you see have a soft focus. If you are sitting, rest your hands by your side or place them on your lap. Some people keep their palms up, others fold their hands. Experiment with what feels best for you.

This meditation asks that you alternate between using two very different parts of your mind. When you breath in, think the words "I'm sorry, please forgive me, thank you, I love you."

When you exhale, do not think! Just be aware of sensations. You will notice that you will become aware of different senses at different times. You may just be aware of the sound of the rain outside, or the sensation of the heat or cold of the day on your skin. You may notice a full or hungry sensation in your belly or the passing air on your nostrils and upper lip as you exhale. And, of course, you will notice you are thinking about something. Ho'oponopono! Forgive yourself automatically and return to your breath.

There will be a short time when you are neither inhaling nor exhaling. Notice that time, as well. This is a time when you are actually not breathing, yet you have faith that soon you will be. Some people report that during these brief moments is when they can most easily experience a oneness with all there is.

# 2. Body Gratitude Meditation

Stay focused on your body and send gratitude to all the things your body does for you. You may choose to start at the top of your head and go down, for instance: Thank you brain, thank you eyes, thank you nose; or start at the soles of your feet and go up: Thank you bottom of my feet, thank you toes, thank you ankles. You may allow different parts of your body to call attention to themselves randomly.

This is a good time to be aware of what's going on in your body. Pay attention. Listen quietly to what your body may be telling you. Every time will be different.

Are there tight places, heavy places, achy or painful places? Accept all the sensations in your body. Give attention to the parts of you that are light and comfortable. Don't worry if you can't focus on specific muscles, relaxing them or even noticing that they are there. Accept yourself and your body just as it is. Put a tiny smile on your face.

Consider the automatic things your body can do, like digesting food and pumping blood. Consider the things you are able to do with your body that bring you happiness, like using your legs and stomach muscles to run, and your hands and arms and sense of rhythm to play the drums. There doesn't have to be a limit to the gratitude you may feel.

If while meditating, you start creating a story in your head about some memory, don't create another one by bawling yourself out for leaving the meditation. Just go back to giving thanks for the gift that you were born in a human body. Don't forget to exhale!

# 3. Square Breathing

We humans breathe about 21,600 times a day! Let's make the way we breathe help us feel comfortable. One of the ways that helps us concentrate on our breathing is sometimes called "square" breathing.

To start, put a hand on your stomach and feel it expand as you breathe in to the count of seven (one, two, three, four, five six, seven). Hold your breath gently to the count of seven. Exhale to the count of seven, contracting your stomach slowly. Gently hold your breath for another seven counts.

Count fast or slowly, whatever feels right in the moment. Don't pressure yourself. Feeling pressure is the opposite of what you want to experience when you're meditating.

In the times when you are holding your breath (gently!), imagine that you are floating in a Sea of Love where stress, worries, anger and sadness do not exist. Imagine everything in the universe being part of that sea, limitless.

When you are floating in this Sea of Love you can remember that you are a part of everything. This is a good time to send love to a part of you that is younger. If, for example, your inner child would like a life jacket while you are in the sea, imagine one and provide it. Feel the sense of comfort and joy that is in your body and mind. You can ask your inner child to help you keep the good feelings.

Repeat the square breathing until your meditation time is up.

When you realize you have wandered away from focusing on your breathing, take a calming breath and say to yourself "I'm sorry, please forgive me, thank you, I love you," (or other words you have chosen), and return to your square breathing. You can coordinate part or all of this mantra with your breathing.

Practice this anytime or all day long. With plenty of practice, you will have an every day tool for the rest of your life. The adult-you will remember and thank the kid-you for all that practice.

# 4. Gazing Meditation

Gazing meditation is very easy. This is a good meditation to do when you only have a few minutes. Try it before taking a test or playing a sport.

Pick any object to gaze at. All the better, choose one that brings you a sense of peace like a flower, a picture or a candle.

Slow your breathing and softly stare, or gaze, at the object. You can blink but don't look away.

It's normal if the object seems to change shape or color. It's normal for difficult feelings or weird thoughts to come up. Just notice whatever happens.

Accept everything and you will notice how, if you don't hold on to them too tightly, the different images, thoughts and feelings leave as easily as they come.

Observe how your breathing gets slower and deeper and how your mind becomes calmer.

Gaze until your meditation time is up.

When you realize you have stopped putting all your attention on gazing, take a calming breath, say to yourself, "I'm sorry, please forgive me, thank you, I love you", and return to gazing.

# 5. Mudra Meditations

Yoga mudras involve placing your fingers in certain positions that can help focus and balance the energies in your body and bring inner peace. Practicing different types of mudras can bring physical, mental and spiritual benefits.

Decide how long you will be meditating. After you have found a comfortable place to sit, relax as you take several square breaths.

You will be matching different finger positions to the words in a mantra. Two of the many choices of phrases to say are *I'm sorry...please forgive me...thank you...I love you, and Peace... begins...with...me.*

Place one or both hands in front of your heart.

- Touch your thumb to your pointer finger and let the words "I'm sorry" or "Peace" come to you.

- Touch your thumb to your middle finger and think or hear the words "Please forgive me" or "begins".

- Touch your thumb to your ring finger and be with the words "Thank you" or "with".

- Touch your thumb to your baby finger and think or hear the words "I love you" or "me".

Repeat until your meditation time is up. When you realize you have wandered away from focusing on the mudras and the words, take a calming breath, immediately forgive yourself and return to the words and the mudras.

# 6. Loving-Kindness Meditation

This is an ancient Tibetan meditation you can use while you sit for a while. It is also a beautiful cleaning tool you can use anywhere and in many situations. It will remind you that you are connected to everyone and everything. Most importantly, it will be a reminder of your own loving, kind heart and your right to be peaceful and happy.

After you have settled yourself comfortably, begin to repeat the following mantra to yourself:

> May I be filled with loving-kindness.
> May I be well.
> May I be peaceful and at ease.
> May I be happy.

Read this until you feel you know it and can keep repeating it. You can repeat it without focusing on anything but the words. You can also allow yourself a little time to imagine your whole being filled with loving-kindness, health, peace, ease and happiness.

It may help to imagine that this loving energy is coming from Divinity to you, as well as to the little child you were. Notice any positive sensations and focus on the feelings for a few seconds.

You may notice that you begin to have kinder feelings about yourself. Even if you aren't positive at first that you can fill yourself with love, just allow yourself to think the words.

The next step is to direct the words to people to whom you feel close and for whom you feel love or gratitude. These could be certain people in your family or a favorite teacher or a best bud. Imagine these people are with you and silently say to them, one at a time:

> May you be filled with loving-kindness.
> May you be well.
> May you be peaceful and at ease.
> May you be happy.

Your next step is to include other people in your community you care about, for instance the kids at school or your neighbors. If particular people come to mind, of course you can hold them in your heart.

Your positive thoughts can then go to all the people you don't know–the people in your city, your county, your state, and country. Keep expanding the group of people until you are imagining all the different people in the world. Continue increasing your well wishes to all the animals, the plants and the earth itself.

This next step is important and may be challenging. Direct your words to difficult-to-like people. These may be people in your life or people you have read about online or in the paper or saw on the history channel. Consider this: if these people were filled with loving kindness, and were well mentally and physically, if they were peaceful and happy, they certainly would be easier to like. Wish them love because they need it the most. It can't hurt.

Next, consider all people, gently repeating the words

> May we be filled with loving-kindness.
> May we be well.
> May we be peaceful and at ease.
> May we be happy.

You may spend your entire meditation directing the words to yourself (May I be..., etc) because you are the most important person to be loving, peaceful and happy. You may also go through all the steps several times. When you realize you have allowed thoughts to distract you from your meditation, take a calming breath and say to yourself, "I'm sorry, please forgive me, thank you, I love you". Return to the loving–kindness mantra.

# 7. Noticing Sounds Meditation

Take a few minutes to notice the noisiness of your thoughts. Most likely you are thinking about the past or the future. One way to quiet down that thought noise is to focus on the sound of yourself breathing in and out. You may want to exaggerate the sound occasionally to get yourself back on track. So feel free to let out a big sigh.

When the inside noises have quieted down, become aware of the sounds outside of yourself. Each sound is in the moment. The future and the past mean nothing to the sounds. So if you are focused on the sounds you can also be in the moment. Before you stop your meditation, listen to yourself breathing again.

# Visualizations

Visualizing is a way to use your creative imagination to relax, to have more energy, and to achieve goals. Visualizations can help you understand yourself better, transform problems, and they can make great cleaning tools! It's fine to share your experiences with other people and it's fine to keep them to yourself.

# 8. Creating a Protective Light

Start with some relaxing, square breathing. Do this several times at your own pace. When you are ready, stop counting and breath naturally.

Imagine a light the size of a seed in the center of your chest. Watch it as it grows with every in-breath and still bigger and brighter with every out-breath.

As you continue to inhale and exhale, you might imagine the light being so big that you are aware of it outside of yourself as well. You might think of yourself as a ball of light or you might just feel this light as a protective, loving energy surrounding you and all your inner children.

When you notice thoughts interrupting your peace, say to yourself, "I'm sorry, please forgive me, thank you, I love you," and return to your breathing and, once again, become aware of the light growing both inside and outside you.

This protective energy is always there. We just need to remind ourselves of its presence. Practice this when you are feeling calm so that it will be second nature to feel this healing light when something stressful happens or whenever you want to feel more confident.

# 9. Visualizing Your Own Special Place

Think of your favorite place to go or be, or, if you want to, you can use your imagination to create a place in your mind that is safe, beautiful and peaceful. It will be totally yours, totally unique. It will be a place you can easily return to whenever you want a moment's relaxation or a half–hour meditation.

Take in a few calming breaths. If you would like, when you exhale, allow yourself to sigh with a sound, like "om" or "ha". Notice parts of your body that feel tight and imagine your in-breath is sending relaxing energy to them and your out-breath is removing tension from them.

Visualize yourself at the beginning of the path that leads to your peaceful place. With each step, allow your body to feel more deeply relaxed. Read the following suggestions, but you don't need to follow them exactly. Start from scratch when you create your own place.

You may imagine your special place to be a beautiful garden, a flowing stream, a meadow, or, perhaps, a spot overlooking the ocean. It could also be your cozy bed or a corner of your backyard, under an oak tree. Is the path narrow or wide? Are there steps and are they made of wood or cement or carved in the dirt? Is it a shady dirt trail winding its way into a forest? Is it a route you always take to a park in your neighborhood?

As you meander into this special place, notice how your senses seem to awaken. Your experience will be different if you are in a forest, near the ocean or in the desert. What kind of trees and flowers do you imagine? What else do you see? If it is a garden, is it well-manicured or is it wild?

Use all your senses. What kinds of sounds do you hear? You may hear birds or a waterfall or the wind whistling through the trees. You may hear waves crashing or complete silence except for the sound of your own breathing.

Are you aware of any scents—perhaps of the nearby ocean or pine needles or the dirt under your feet?

Feel the air on your skin. Is it warm or cool? Is there a breeze? Is your body becoming more relaxed or is there a place in your body that needs some gentle attention?

Create a place to sit and rest. You may be using this seating in the future, so make it comfy. It could be a beautiful wooden bench, or a giant soft pillow, or perhaps it it's a spot on the grass under a tree or somewhere fun, like a playground or a theme park.

Invite your Inner Divinity to join you in your special place. He or she may come as a grandparent, your basketball coach, a fairy godmother or an angel. It may be a glowing ball of light, two outstretched hands, or the night sky. You may not have an image, but a sense of a very comforting and loving energy.

Take a few calming breaths. Tell your Inner Divinity what struggles you're having. And listen. Become very quiet and listen longer. You may hear a quiet, gentle voice offering the guidance you need.

Spend all the time you need in your peaceful place and let good feelings fill your heart. You can walk out the way you came or return in an instant to your everyday world. You can go to the peace of this special, unique sanctuary every time you meditate.

## 10. Creating Sculptures

This visualization makes good use of your magnificent imagination. Begin by imagining that you have a beautiful park in your back yard, and want to create a sculpture to express a problem in your life. After finding a quiet place to meditate, find a comfortable place in your park to relax, close your eyes and just be. You are here to let go so that Inspiration will visit you and you can make the exact sculpture you want.

In a little while, take a moment to think about a problem in your life. Check in to see if any of your inner children shares this problem with you.

What are the thoughts and feelings you have about the problem? Listen for clues in your body that help identify the feelings. Is your throat tight? It your chest heavy? Are there butterflies in your stomach or tears in your eyes?

Spend some time designing the sculpture of your problem. Decide how big you want it to be. Decide what it is made of, if it is hot or cold, smooth or prickly or squishy, and what color it is. Does it have parts that move? Do you want to let people touch or climb on it, or do you want a fence or a moat around it?

Look at it from all sides. If it is bigger than you, imagine a ladder or drone that enables you to see it from above. What is the name of your sculpture?

Now, for the fun part. Since you are the owner of the park and of the sculpture you made, you and your magnificent imagination can let all sorts of magical workers and artists transform it.

Think about what the sculpture might look like if the situation became less of a problem. For instance, if the sculpture shows that the pain in your broken toe feels hot to you, your workers may pack snow on it to make it cooler. If your sculpture expresses anger, they may soften and smooth the jagged edges just by their loving touch.. Perhaps you would like the sculpture to be taken to the dump or rocketed to the sun. You're the boss!

Before you finish this meditation, take a few deep breaths and thank your imagination and its imaginary magical workers. Come back to your sculpture park anytime and make any changes you think are needed. The park is as huge as your imagination and you can create as many sculptures as you want, whenever you want.

## 11. Sweeping Out the Dirt

Imagine a pile of dirt is inside your skull. The dirt is the stuff that you've been having trouble let go of—like anger, blame or fear. Take long breaths in and let them out slowly. Your breath can be like a warm wind blowing the dirt out through invisible vents in your skull. You don't have to know exactly what is being cleaned away, but you may want to be specific. You can ask the wind to, for instance, blow away your fear of standing in front of a class, or worries that you won't be able to remember what you studied for a math test or think you have to be right and that your only choice is to stay mad at someone. You can sweep for ten seconds or twenty minutes!

# *Part Three*

## Many Teachers

*(Please note: Where applicable, all quotes are the copyright of their respective owners.)*

### Ho'oponopono is about

### ENERGY

*E*nergy is everything – It's the essence of life!
~Anthon St. Maarten

Forgiveness is required to dissolve all the negative energy cords because it releases shame, guilt, anger, hatred, etc.
~Hina Hashmi,

There are only two kinds of people who can drain your energy: those you love, and those you fear. In both instances it is you who let them in. They did not force their way into your aura, or pry their way into your reality experience.
~Jonathan Talat Phillips

Energy healing is like defragmenting your hard drive. The scattered pieces of yourself become whole again.
~Elaine Seiler

The energy of life entering and leaving your body flows evenly throughout the universe. With that current, the mind of the cosmos communicates with all things.
~Lynne McTaggart

When we came into the world we had agreement to vibrate at a certain energy. When we hold on to negative thoughts and feelings, we disturb our energy field and so the entire energy of the universe. Forgiving someone doesn't mean that we condone their behavior. The act of forgiveness takes place in our own mind. It really has nothing to do with the other person. The reality of true forgiveness lies in setting ourselves free from holding on to the pain. It's simply an act of releasing ourselves from the negative energy.
~Louise Hay

If you want to find the secrets of the universe, think in terms of energy, frequency and vibration.
~Ilchi Lee

We are all connected: To each other, biologically. To the earth, chemically. To the rest of the universe, atomically.
~Nikola Tesla

I define connection as the energy that exists between people when they feel seen, heard and valued; when they can give and receive without judgment; and when they derive sustenance and strength from the relationship.
~Neil deGrasse Tyson

We live as ripples of energy in the vast ocean of energy.
~Toba Beta

The whole universe appears as a dynamic web of inseparable energy patterns…Thus we are not separated parts of a whole. We are a Whole.
~Barbara Ann Brennan

It does not matter how long you are spending on the earth, how much money you have gathered or how much attention you have received. It is the amount of positive vibration you have radiated in life that matters.
~Amit Ray

Love is the energy from which all people and things are made. You are connected to everything in your world through love.
~Brian L Weiss, M.D.

Luke: The Force? Ben: Now, the Force is what gives a Jedi his power. It's an energy field created by all living things. It surrounds us, it penetrates us, it binds the galaxy together.
~Conversation in Star Wars, 1977, Lucasfilms

A Prayer to the Never-ending Field of Infinite Energy:
I am sorry that I have disturbed your peaceful energy. Please forgive me so that anything that has been disturbed may find peace. Thank you for mending broken connections in the web of infinite energy of which I am a part. Thank you for giving me the opportunity to experience life in a human body and to clean. I love you and offer my energy to blend peacefully into your infinite energy.
-Katrina Clover

# Ho'oponopono is about
# **MEDITATION**

Meditation is not a way of making your mind quiet. It's a way of entering into the quiet that's already there - buried under the 50,000 thoughts the average person thinks every day.
~ Deepak Chopra

Meditation applies the brakes to the mind.
~ Ramana Maharshi

No matter how strange things get, know that with every breath, you are becoming that which you have always been.
~Eric Micha'el Leventhal

Before embarking on important undertakings, sit quietly, calm your senses and thoughts and meditate deeply. You will then be guided by the great creative power of Spirit.
~Paramahansa Yogananda

If a person's basic state of mind is serene and calm, then it is possible for this inner peace to overwhelm a painful physical experience.
~Dalai Lama

It is better to conquer yourself than to win a thousand battles. Then the victory is yours. It cannot be taken from you, not by angels or by demons, heaven or hell.
~Buddha

Remember to breath. It is after all, the secret of life.
~Gregory Maguire

*MEDITATION*

Mind is a door that leads you outside in the world; meditation is the door that leads you to your interiority - to the very innermost shrine of your being.
~Bhagwan Shree Rajneesh

To meet everything and everyone through stillness instead of mental noise is the greatest gift you can offer the universe.
~Eckhart Tolle

Breath is the bridge which connects life to consciousness, which unites your body to your thoughts. Whenever your mind becomes scattered, use your breath as the means to take hold of your mind again.
~Thich Nhat Hanh

Your goal is not to battle with the mind, but to witness the mind.
~Swami Muktananda

In meditation you are not unconscious, you are conscious - more conscious than ever.
~Bhagwan Shree Rajneesh

Meditation is the ultimate mobile device; you can use it anywhere, anytime, unobtrusively.
~Sharon Salzberg

Be still and know.
~Aristotle

# Ho'oponopono is about
# RESPONSIBILITY

I am only here for one purpose–only to make amends. My job is to be 100% responsible and do the cleaning. My only purpose is to let go so I can be free.
~Dr. I Hew Len

We are taking responsibility when we apologize and ask for forgiveness. This is not taking the blame or assuming that we have done something wrong.
~Dr. I Hew Len

Wherever you are, be there totally. If you find your here-and-now intolerable and it makes you unhappy, you have three options: remove yourself from the situation, change it or accept it totally. If you want to take responsibility for your life, you must choose one of those three options, and you must choose now. Then accept the consequences.
~Eckhart Tolle

No one saves us but ourselves. No one can and no one may. We ourselves must walk the path.
~Buddha

The greatest day in your life and mine is when we take total responsibility for our attitudes. That's the day we truly grow up.
~John C. Maxwell

You must take personal responsibility. You cannot change the circumstances, the season, or the wind, but you can change yourself. That is something you have charge of.
~Jim Rohn

*RESPONSIBILITY*

We are made wise not by the recollection of our past, but by the responsibility for our future.
~George Bernard Shaw

Find joy in everything you choose to do. Every job, relationship, home... it's your responsibility to love it, or change it.
~Chuck Palahniuk

Take full responsibility for yourself, for the time you take up and the space you occupy. If you don't know what you're here to do, then just do some good.
~Maya Angelou

One's philosophy is not best expressed in words; it is expressed in the choices one makes and the choices we make are ultimately our responsibility.
~Eleanor Roosevelt

"When a man points a finger at someone else, he should remember that four of his fingers are pointing at himself."
~Louis Nizer, a well-known American lawyer

"A man can fail many times, but he isn't a failure until he begins to blame somebody else."
~John Burroughs

# Ho'oponopono is about
# LETTING GO

Forgiveness is not always easy. At times, it feels more painful than the wound we suffered, to forgive the one that inflicted it. And yet, there is no peace without forgiveness.
~Marianne Williamson

Holding on to anger is like grasping a hot coal with the intent of throwing it at someone else but you are the one who gets burned.
You will not be punished for your anger, you will be punished by your anger.
~Buddha, 500 BC

As human beings we all want to be happy and free from misery. We have learned that the key to happiness is inner peace. The greatest obstacles to inner peace are disturbing emotions such as anger and attachment, fear and suspicion, while love and compassion, a sense of universal responsibility are the sources of peace and happiness.
~Dalai Lama

Those who pardon and maintain righteousness are rewarded by God. He does not love the unjust.
~Qur'an 42:40

Oh Divine Master, grant that I may not so much seek to be consoled as to console. To be understood as to understand. To be loved as to love. For it is in giving that we receive. It is in pardoning that we are pardoned. And it is in dying that we are born to eternal life.

~St. Francis of Assisi

Judge not, and ye shall not be judged: condemn not, and ye shall not be condemned: forgive, and ye shall be forgiven.
~Luke 6:37 KJV

The superior man tends to forgive wrongs and deals leniently with crimes.
~I Ching 40: Release

Forgiveness is a virtue of the brave.
~Indira Gandhi

The weak can never forgive. Forgiveness is the attribute of the strong.
~Mahatma Gandhi

The best deed of a great man is to forgive and forget.
~Nahjul Balagha

Where there is forgiveness, there is God Himself.
~Kabir

Who takes vengeance or bears a grudge acts like one who, having cut one hand while handling a knife, avenges himself by stabbing the other hand.
~Jerusalem Talmud, Nedarim 9.4

Forgiveness is the fragrance that the violet sheds on the heel that has crushed it.
~Mark Twain

To forgive is to set a prisoner free and discover that the prisoner was you.
~Lewis B. Smedes

# Ho'oponopono is about
# GRATITUDE

Thanks for showing up so I have one more chance to clean memories.
~Hew Len to "the enemy" (or negative thoughts)

Concentrate on finding what is good in every situation and you will discover that your life will suddenly be filled with gratitude, a feeling that nurtures the soul.
~Rabbi Harold Kushner

If the only prayer you say in your whole life is "thank you," that would suffice.
~Meister Eckhart

Gratitude is like a flashlight. If you go out in your yard at night and turn on a flashlight, you suddenly can see what's there. It was always there, but you couldn't see it in the dark.
~Dawna Markova

At times our own light goes out and is rekindled by a spark from another person. Each of us has cause to think with deep gratitude on those who have lighted the flame within us.
~Albert Schweitzer

The road to happiness starts with a deep breath and an awareness of the many blessings tied to that single breath.
~Richelle E. Goodrich

As we express our gratitude, we must never forget that the highest appreciation is not to utter words, but to live by them.
~John F. Kennedy

# GRATITUDE

This is what binds all people and all creation together—the gratitude of the gift of being.
~Matthew Fox

Gratitude is not only the greatest of virtues, but the parent of all others.
~Cicero

In our daily lives, we must see that it is not happiness that makes us grateful, but gratefulness that makes us happy.
~Albert Clark

Be thankful for what you have; you'll end up having more. If you concentrate on what you don't have, you will never, ever have enough.
~Oprah Winfrey

Piglet noticed that even though he had a Very Small Heart, it could hold a rather large amount of Gratitude.
~A.A. Milne

Forget yesterday–it has already forgotten you. Don't sweat tomorrow--you haven't even met. Instead, open your eyes and you heart to a truly precious gift–today.
~Steve Maraboli

# Ho'oponopono is about
# LOVE

*We can have love for a parent, a child, a friend, or a pet. We can love our city or a favorite baseball team. We can have romantic love for a girlfriend or boyfriend.*

*Ho'oponopono refers to the love we have for and receive from Divinity. It also refers to the love we have for expressions of the Divine - ourselves, humanity, the animal world, plants and the earth. Ho'oponopono love reminds us that we are all one and there is no separation between us and Divinity.*

\*\*\*

All major religious traditions carry essentially the same message, that is one of love, compassion and forgiveness. The important thing is they should be part of our daily lives.
~Dalai Lama

Thou shalt love thy neighbour as thyself.
~Matthew 22:39 KJV

If you judge people, you have no time to love them.
~Mother Teresa

Your task is not to seek for love, but merely to see and find all the barriers within yourself that you have built against it.
~Rumi

Love is how it feels to recognize our essential unity. Awakening to oneness is the experience of Big Love. Knowing you are one with all, you find yourself in love with all.
~Timothy Freke

When there is love in your heart, everything outside of you also becomes lovable.
~Veeresh

Only through love can we obtain communion with God.
~Albert Schweitzer

You are not a drop in the ocean
You are the entire ocean in a drop.
~Rumi

When we try to pick out anything by itself, we find it hitched to everything else in the Universe.
~John Muir

But love ye your enemies, and do good, and lend, hoping for nothing again; and your reward shall be great, and ye shall be the children of the Highest: for he is kind unto the unthankful and to the evil.
~Luke 6:35 KJV

This is my simple religion. There is no need for temples; no need for complicated philosophy. Our own brain, our own heart is our temple; the philosophy is kindness.
~Dalai Lama

"I was six when I saw that everything was God, and my hair stood up, and all," Teddy said. "It was on a Sunday, I remember. My sister was a tiny child then, and she was drinking her milk, and all of a sudden I saw that she was God and the milk was God. I mean, all she was doing was pouring God into God, if you know what I mean."
~J.D. Salinger, Teddy, 1953

You, yourself, as much as anybody in the entire universe, deserves your love and affection.
~Buddha

We are completely woven out of each other and the cosmos itself.
~Rev. James Ishmael Ford

And as ye would that men should do to you, do ye also to them likewise.
~Luke 6:31 KJV

If you want others to be happy, practice compassion.
If you want to be happy, practice compassion.
~Dalai Lama

I honor the place in you in which the entire universe dwells.
I honor the place in you, which is of love, of truth, of light and of peace.
When you are in that place in you, and I am in that place in me, we are one.
~Ancient Namaste prayer
("namaste" means "I bow to you")

# DR. IHALEAKALA HEW LEN
# ON HO'OPONOPONO

*The psychologist, Dr. Hew Len, is a beloved teacher of Ho'oponopono. The following quotes are taken from talks by and interviews with Dr. Hew Len on Youtube; his book with Dr. Joe Vitale, Zero Limits; and his website, zero-wise.com.*

In the beginning, when we were initially created, we were nothing - blank, no data, perfect in every way. We didn't have to think or make money.

There was no data playing. From that 'no data', the void, comes enlightenment. The source of that light, for some reason, decided to create each one of us.

Each of us is infinitely zero. That means we can experience heaven on earth, through art and painting and love. So that's how we began.

Each of us is given a gift of this lifetime: "To thy own self be true."

We are an exact likeness of the divine, zero, infinite.

Zero means to be empty, free. At zero, you're free from whatever's going on in your life. There's nothing outside yourself. All the info in you is already there. That information is what you have brought into this lifetime. The idea is very simple - if you are at Zero, everybody else will be at zero. Zero begins with you.

When you look with the eyes of the Divine, you will see only love in people.

We are in a grand symphony. Each of has an instrument to play. None are the same. In order for the concert to play and everyone to enjoy it, they need to play their part and not another's.

We get into trouble when we don't pick up our instrument or we think someone has a better one. That's memory.

Everything holds memories...there is nothing that does not hold memories...all your problems are memories replaying.

All the memories in you are in everything.

Ho'oponopono is done entirely within yourself. You don't have to know what the problem or error is. All you have to do is notice. Once you notice, your responsibility is to immediately begin to clean, to say, "I'm sorry. Please forgive me."

We spend all our lives trying to persuade people instead of being in love.

I simply clean the part of me that I share [with other people].

It [Ho'oponopono] is only about the cleaning.

# The Old Man and the White Horse

*This is an ancient story, taught by Lao Tzu, founder of the Chinese philosophy of Taoism in the 6th century BC. It reminds us to take each moment as it comes, without judgment, and not to assume that we can know the future.*

Many years ago, in a remote village in China, there lived a poor man and his family. One day, a beautiful white horse walked into his yard. Many of his neighbors came to see this fine horse and congratulate him. "What a great and wonderful thing to happen!", they declared. "You are so lucky. With this horse, you are now a wealthy man!"

The man replied in a calm voice, "Friends, I do not choose to see this as good or bad. The horse came into my yard. He is a beautiful horse that I am beginning to love like a member of my family. That is all." The people scratched their heads and left, wondering about the sanity of their friend.

A few weeks later, the man looked in his yard and could not find the horse. His neighbors came over to console him. "Old man", they declared. "We are so sorry for you. You have lost that magnificent horse. What terrible luck."

To this, the man responded, in his wise and peaceful manner, "Friends, again you tell me how I should react to this situation. I am not sad, I am not miserable. The horse is not in the yard. This is not good nor bad. The horse is not here. Take care, my friends. Good bye." Again his neighbors left in wonderment and sadness that their friend was going crazy.

Several weeks later, the man awoke early in the morning, to hear a racket outside his little house. The commotion was made by the chattering of his friends because, there in his yard, was his white horse and two more, just as magnificent!

As usual, his neighbors were ready to tell him the nature of his experience and how he should feel. "Old man, you are the luckiest person in the land. You must be thrilled; you have three beautiful horses. Your son can train them and when you sell them you will be richer that anyone in five provinces. This is so wonderful!"

True to himself, the old man repeated his mantra.

"It is what it is," he said. "I have three horses. I will not think it good or great or thrilling. I now have three beautiful horses. They are in my yard at this moment. Thank you for caring, my friends. Good day." His neighbors left, muttering their disbelief of their friend's attitude.

Life was calm in the village for several weeks. The old man's son spent many hours training the three beautiful horses. One afternoon he fell off the largest one and broke both legs. The neighbors came to visit when they heard the news.

"Oh, such terrible news. You must be feeling so, so sad. You have these horses, but with these broken legs, there is no one able to train them. Such a misfortune!"

This time, the son spoke.

"Friends, we are grateful that we have such caring neighbors. But this is not terrible nor a misfortune. It need not be a cause for sadness. I have broken legs. Period. It is what it is and nothing more."

This time, the neighbors left whispering to each other about how, now, the old man's son was a fool.

The last part of this story need not be the end. One can imagine many more events in the old man's life that may or may not be called good or bad.

The young man's legs did not heal very fast. His father took good care of him, as did their caring neighbors, who also helped with the horses. One day, several soldiers came to the old man's house. They explained that their country and the adjoining country had declared a war against each other. These soldiers were even going to this remote village to sign up every able-bodied man to go to war. When they caught sight of the old man's son lying on the bed, with pillows under his heavily wrapped leg, they apologized and left the house. When the neighbors heard about this event, they were, for once, finally, quiet.

# *Part Four*

# The Psychotherapeutic Connection

## The Author's Journey

*O*NE of life's joys and intrigues is the investigation of truth and meaning. The exploration of the world's religions can bring us closer to our own answers, and through my own studies, I've seen that the principles of Ho'oponopono are woven throughout most religions. It is as if their most essential messages of infinite love, forgiveness, gratitude, and personal responsibility have been distilled into one practice, based on a simple understanding of our place in the universe.

I have found in Ho'oponopono, primarily through the teachings of Ihaleakala Hew Len, an elegant explanation of our human existence and purpose that makes sense to me. Ho'oponopono suits me, especially, because of its simplicity. It does not rely on an official instruction book (and books about that book), nor does it rely on other people. It does rely on each of us making a conscious decision to walk through life on a Ho'oponopono path, and to take responsibility and forgive ourselves when we invariably stray off that path.

The practice of Ho'oponopono offers a gentle way, without sacrificing religious beliefs, to be open to answers. Reflections of these connections can be found in the quotes in the "Ho'oponopono is ..." chapters of this book.

When I began my career as a Marriage and Family Therapist in the late eighties, I doubted 'spirituality' belonged in the psychotherapy office at all. I am taken with how limited my definition of spirituality was then. I equated spirituality with religion, and, with it, a bully pulpit which limited the questioning of its dogma and did not respect different lifestyles and personal beliefs.

Now I equate spirituality with energy, with quantum mind, with healing and with love. It brings to mind being-in-the-moment and Oneness. After thousands of hours using energy therapies, coming from both mind and heart, and learning to trust my intuition, I have come to the perspective that it is only through the energy of spirit that healing manifests completely.

Since my earliest days as an intern, I have treated adults recovering from the abuse in their childhoods. This includes several clients, raised or influenced by cults, who had been intentionally and incessantly abused. The topic is not appropriate content for a children's book, but suffice it to say that it is not unusual for the mind of a child in this situation to develop a wonderfully creative coping strategy. In her brilliant mind, she creates new parts of herself, essentially new identities, to handle the abuse. She is then able to block out, or dissociate, personal awareness of the frightening and degrading situation.

I would not have written about Dakota's journey had I not had the honor of journeying with these brave souls as they explored their own minds. Spiritual injuries must be met with spiritual healing. Walking with these people for my small part of their healing journey has been a powerful introduction to the most transcendent capacities of our consciousness.

As an intern, I was fascinated when, at a conference at UC Berkeley in 1988, I heard a talk by Dr. Francine Shapiro about her new therapeutic tool, now referred to as EMDR (Eye Movement Desensitization and Reprocessing, EMD at the time). Very briefly, EMDR combines crossing the body bilaterally (using the eyes, ears, touch or movement) while focusing on distressing thoughts, feelings and imagery. EMDR clinicians use SUDs measures, (subjective units of distress), before and after treatment. In this way, both my clients and I are often able to see the astounding effectiveness in releasing their stuck feelings and negative self-definition. I didn't define it as such then, but I began using energy psychology in 1990.

As challenging as the complexity of the mind can be, I am grateful to have had the good fortune to study hypnosis and consult with Dr. Tony Madrid. In a process that emphasizes safety, respect and integrity, I have been able to guide my clients deep into their subconscious mind and beyond, to what some refer to as the Superconscious or Inner Wisdom. This part of all of us has an instant connection to Divinity, or, if you will, magic and miracles. The imagery I have of the mind has been formed over countless sessions of hypnosis with a diversity of people. In session, their inner wisdom and my intuition collaborate, so that their unconscious memories, thoughts, beliefs, and feelings can be retrieved, transformed and let go.

Thanks to the internet, I was introduced to EFT about the same time I discovered Ho'oponopono. Emotional Freedom Technique was founded by Gary Craig, who had been a student of Roger Callhan's Thought Field Therapy. Briefly, EFT involves tapping on energy meridians, similar to those used in acupuncture, while thinking and voicing the many aspects and feelings about a problem. This is always coupled with positive affirmations regarding the person's ability to be self-loving, self-accepting and self-forgiving. Unlike EMDR, non-therapists are encouraged to learn EFT and use it on themselves as often as needed.

My religious affiliation, Unitarian Universalism, professes no dogma, but offers seven principles that we affirm and promote, beginning with the first principle–the inherent worth and dignity of every person. The seventh principle is respect for the interconnected web of existence, of which we all are a part. These are just two of a myriad of ways to acknowledge Divinity.

However, it was not until my introduction to Ho'oponopono, that I realized that I, as a psychotherapist, was buying into a dynamic of "me and them," with my clients. As a therapist I've had the opportunity, thanks to EMDR, EFT, hypnosis, slo-mo-pono, and the energy of trust and love, to witness thousands of healing experiences and mini-miracles in my office. I am now viscerally aware that I am primarily the one being healed.

I introduce some of the concepts of Ho'oponopono to most of my clients in their first or second session. I explain that I see almost everything with an overlay of Ho'oponopono and that I may, in our work together, point out the Ho'oponopono perspective in a situation. I point to the essentials of self–love, 100% responsibility (avoiding blame and victimization) and forgiveness.

My clients are often encouraged to consider what it is that they would like to let go of during a session. This question shifts the emphasis from a sense of powerlessness regarding problems, to a sense of personal responsibility to let go. The use of EFT and EMDR almost invariably results in a release of toxic or self-defeating thoughts and feelings.

"Slo-mo-pono," as described in this book, honors the relationship of my clients with their younger, more vulnerable selves, points to the thoughts that create problems, and encourages clients' relationships with their Inner and Greater Divinities. Finally, it can dramatically and somewhat magically demonstrate the Ho'oponopono transmutation process. Another activity that has been valuable to both young and older clients is one that involves "Caca Mountain". After drawing the simple outline of a mountain, help the client (child, friend or yourself) designate sections, in pencil, that identify thoughts and feelings that are bothersome. Then, eraser in hand, the owner of this Caca Mountain erases each section, at the same time saying out loud or internally, a cleaning mantra. This often creates a dramatic letting go, not only intellectually but physically and emotionally.

Some of my clients express gratitude for the introduction to Ho'oponopono, incorporating this practice immediately and reporting on significant changes in their relationships and, especially, within themselves. Others are not interested in the subject, and I clean on my own disappointment, frustration and egoic attitude. Ultimately, healing does not come from my persuading people to use the principles of Ho'oponopono. My job as a psychotherapist is to recognize and correct my own erroneous thoughts, to replace them with the healing power of love, and to get out of the way of Divine Inspiration (God, Love, etc.).

# Psychotherapeutic Approaches to Ho'oponopono

Just as the principles of Ho'oponopono are woven into the fabric of the world's religions, they also may be found in a variety of contemporary psychotherapies. These approaches are found in the teachings of transpersonal and existential psychology, as well as stemming from trauma theory, family systems and cognitive behavioral theory.

When I discovered Ho'oponopono, I found a simple way to help my clients, and myself, with mindfulness practice. I often use meditation, guided visualizations and hypnosis to guide them in becoming more relaxed and present in their bodies. As a psychotherapeutic modality, mindfulness helps us return to the moment and observe thoughts and feelings from a distance, without judging them as good or bad. This therapeutic practice is reflected in the Ho'oponopono invitation to continually release thoughts connected to the past or the future.

Transpersonal psychotherapy attempts to identify and study consciousness, and give us the option to move comfortably between the conscious mind, the subconscious and the superconscious. One aspect of this therapy, found in many Buddhist teachings, is this mindfulness, a state of active, open attention on the present.

While exploring the challenges and paradoxes of human existence, existential therapy emphasizes, as does Ho'oponopono, that we are free to make our own choices and that we, ultimately, must take responsibility for all of them. We, and our lives, are defined by these choices.

Another psychotherapeutic approach is cognitive behavioral therapy. A centerpiece of Ho'oponopono is the focus on the present. Just as one would find this in mindfulness practice, so it is found in CBT. Considering the idea that our emotions are a reflection of how we perceive situations, cognitive behavioral therapy offers a variety of options to identify distorted thinking and behaviors to address mistakes. Rather than analyzing thoughts, however, Ho'oponopono explains that all our negative thoughts stem from memories, and offers one powerful behavioral change: that of letting go, or cleaning, any negative thought or emotion connected to a memory.

Ho'oponopono is reflected in the family systems approach to therapy. Individuals cannot be understood in isolation from one another, but rather as a part of their family. Similarly, we need not see ourselves separate from any part of our bodies or psyche, our families and ancestors, nature, or our Source. Healing is more likely to occur when not only the "Identified Patient", but everyone in the family, acknowledges his or her responsibility for the problems.

Within any relational therapy, and especially family therapy, a most useful practice is to have each member present complete the sentences in the mantra: I'm sorry...[for the pain that the other person has]; Please forgive me [for the part of the problem that is my responsibility and its consequences]; Thank you [for the positive parts of the relationship]; I love you [especially for or when...]. This process helps the person to stay in the moment, drop blame and drama, accept responsibility, and celebrate love and gratitude.

In trauma therapy, it is essential to become adept at listening to an inner witness or observing self. It is also important to pay attention to the parts of the body that have held on to the trauma.

Using Ho'oponopono cleaning tools, clients can learn to relate not only to their healthiest self, but, with compassion, to specific parts of their bodies and to various ages and aspects of themselves. The more a client can let go of toxic memories, negative self-beliefs, and emotional discomfort in the body, the less power the trauma has to diminish the quality of that person's life. Ho'oponopono can bring a sense of love and joy into the therapeutic setting that, for this author, increasingly adds energy and enthusiasm for the work.

# RESOURCES

## HO'OPONOPONO

There are scary looking clowns and there are friendly clowns. The friendly clowns do good when they make people laugh. Then there are people who live their lives as clowns.

Wavy Gravy is one of those most special clowns. He has worked for peace and justice most of his life and mostly as a clown. Some people call him a hippie clown. He is one of the founders of the Seva Foundation and, along with his wife, Jahanara Romney, created Camp Winnarainbow, where kids learn all kinds of circus skills and how to get along. You will learn all about him in the movie about his life: *Saint Misbehavin': The Wavy Gravy Movie*.

DeNoyelles, Alaya, The Sovereignty of Love, Coming Home With Ho'oponopono, 2012

Dupree, Ulrich E, Ho'oponopono: The Hawaiian Forgiveness Ritual as the Key to Your Life's Fulfillment, 2012

Hew Len, Dr. Ihaleakala and Vitale, Dr.Joe, Zero Limits, 2008

Hew Len, Dr. Ihaleakala and Rafaelo, Kamaile BLUE ICE: The Relationship with The Self, 2014

Youtube: Ho'oponopono Dr. Hew Len and Joe Vitale parts 1-4
Dr. Hew Len profound interview
Dr. Hew Len 1through 9 ho'oponopono (2009)
Mabel Katz website: M Katz interviews Dr. Hew Len

Katz, Mabel, The Easiest Way 2004, The Easiest Way to understanding Ho'oponopono 2009, The Easiest Way to Grow 2011

Lee, Pali Jae Ho'opono The Hawaiian Way to Put Things Back in Balance 2006

# EMOTIONAL FREEDOM TECHNIQUE - TAPPING

A phobia of clowns is just one of the problems that have been treated by EFT, or tapping. This simple and very effective technique can be a powerful cleaning tool for whatever stresses you may have may have.

The internet offers a wealth of EFT sessions demonstrated by generous EFT practitioners who, thanks in great part to the mentoring and modeling of Gary Craig, feel passionate about sharing it. Adults, do these with your kids. Kids, do these with your folks or at least make sure they know you are on the internet. Begin with the **'Gary Craig Official EFT Tutorial'.**

Anthony, Joseph - to get started, google 'Tapping for Teens, The World Needs You' and 'EFT and Curing the Homework Blues'.

Muccillo, Angie,Tapping for Kids: A Children's Guide to Emotional Freedom Technique, 2008

Ortner, Nick, Jessica and Alex. Start by googling Ortner, An Introduction to Tapping; The Tapping Solution for Parents, Children and Teenagers by Nick Ortner; My Magic Breath: Finding Calm Through Mindful Breathing by Nick Ortner and Allison Taylor; Gorilla Thumps and Bear Hugs by Alex Ortner.

Yates, Brad has great videos about tapping on anger and fear. Google 'Yates,Tapping for Kids'. He reads his book on youtube: The Wizard's Wish: Or, How He Made the Yuckies Go Away-A Story About the Magic in You, July, 2010. A Garden of Emotions, Cultivating Peace Through Tapping, 2018.

# MEDITATION, SPIRITUALITY AND PRAYER

## FOR YOUNG CHILDREN

Gates, Mariam, Good Night Yoga: A Pose-by-Pose Bedtime Story

Hanh, Thich Nhat, A Handful of Quiet:Happiness in Four Pebbles

Maclean, Kerry Lee, Peaceful Piggy Meditation

Silver, Gail, Anh's Anger

Snel, Eline, Sitting Still Like a Frog, Mindfulness Exercises for Kids (and Their Parents)

## ESPECIALLY FOR TEENS

Braden, Gregg - among many others: Secrets of the Lost Mode of Prayer Hay House, Inc.2006

Canfield, Jack - in particular: Chicken Soup for the Soul: Just for Teenagers: 101 Stories of Inspiration and Support for Teens, 2011 and Chicken Soup for the Soul: Just for Preteens, 2011

Chopra, Deepak - among over eighty books: Teens Ask Deepak: All the Right Questions 2006 and Fire in the Heart: A Spiritual Guide for Teens, 2006

DiOrio, Rana, What Does It Mean To Be Present? 2010, - for the little kid in all of us.

Dyer, Wayne - just one of over thirty books: <u>10 Secrets for Success and Inner Peace For Teens,</u> 2004

Gawain, Shakti: <u>Creative Visualization,</u> 1982

Lozoff, Bo, <u>We're All Doing Time: a guide for getting free,</u> 1985

Nagaraja, Dharmachari, <u>Buddha at Bedtime: Tales of Love and Wisdom,</u> 2008

Nhat Hanh, Thich - has written many wonderful books of teachings and poetry, for example <u>A Handful of Quiet: Happiness in Four Pebbles,</u> 2012

Ram Dass - has written many important easy to read spiritual books, beginning with <u>Be Here Now,</u> 1971. Take advantage of his teachings through his many books and the internet. *Imagine Meditation, Ram Dass*, available on youtube, is a special meditation, originally presented in 1971. His "last book" (as he has defined it), written with Mirabai Bush is <u>Walking Each Other Home: Conversations on Loving and Dying.</u>

# Gratitudes

My deep gratitude goes

To Dr. Ihaleakala Hew Len. Thank you for having the courage, passion and generosity to share ho'oponopono with the international community.

To Dr. Joe Vitale. Thank you for your inspiring persistence that brought the world the teachings of Dr. Hew Len.

To Dr. Antonio Madrid. Tony, thank you for sharing your perspective of hypnosis. It gave me the beginning of an understanding of the subconscious mind and guidance in accessing the Inner Wisdom.

To Steve Olglivie. Thank you for showing me, in so many ways, the incredible abilities of the mind. Thank you for all your generous teachings and for saving so many lives.

To my clients with dissociated and those with retrieved identities who have trusted me to connected with their inner parts, many hidden for decades. Thank you for the spiritual teachings you have gifted me. It has been an honor.

My psychotherapy clients are usually introduced to ho'oponopono on their first or second session. Thank you to all who were willing to see their lives through the lens of ho'oponopono and experience the transmutation available through slo-mo-pono. You are my teachers and healers!

Writing this book has been an adventure. Six months after I began, I mistakenly thought I was finished. Four years later, still looking at life with the lens of ho'oponopono, I continue to be inspired by new perspectives and ways to share its gifts.

I have been gifted with feedback from many people who have read and commented on one of about twenty iterations of this book. Although you may not recognize it in its present form, please know that your kind and wise support of this humble project continues to be deeply appreciated. My sincere gratitude to Andrew Hidas, Cecilia Lopez, Christie Noe, David Templeton, Drew Tepping, Jan Ogren, Jenny Meeker, Linda Lambert, Logan Lumetta, Luca Lumetta, Lyric Ramos, and Morgan Lambert.

There have also been folk who may have only commented on some aspect of the book. Sometimes those brief communications brought me to a new and invaluable perspective of ho'oponopono. My heartfelt thanks goes to Barbara Zook...Barrie Noe...Charly Hill...Cherie Eliz Ford...Deborah Mason...Deborah Wiig...Ellen Skagerberg...Ian Mutz...Jennifer Horne...Jenny Meeker...Jim Pretorius...Judy Oversby...Ken Wade...Lanie Abrams...Marc Fine...Rachel Wheless...Richard Hillman...Ruth Ann Midi... Samantha Gray...Sandra Novia...Sara Jones...Scott Horne... Sharon Curry...Shonnie Brown...Sidnee Cox...Snow Collins... Sue Wade...Vlatka Herzberg, and participants in the MUGGS, Youth, Adult religious education, and womens retreaters of the Unitarian Universalist Congregation, Santa Rosa.

To those whose support has not been acknowledged here, I am truly sorry. Please forgive me if my neglect has caused you any distress. Feel free to let me know. Thank you for the help you did give me. I love you.

My undying gratitude goes to you, Brian. Your ability to love, let go and forgive inspires me daily.

www.ingramcontent.com/pod-product-compliance
Lightning Source LLC
Chambersburg PA
CBHW030435290526
45786CB00001B/295